PERSPECTIVES ON A GLOBAL GREEN NEW DEAL

Curated by Harpreet Kaur Paul & Dalia Gebrial

Illustration by Tomekah George

Funded by the Federal Ministry for Economic Cooperation
and Development of the Federal Republic of Germany. This
publication or parts of it can be used by others for free as long
as they provide a proper reference to the original publication
including referencing both the curators and editors as well as
any individual contributing authors as relevant.

Legally responsible for the publication: Tsafrir Cohen, Director,
Regional Office UK & Ireland, Rosa Luxemburg Stiftung.

ISBN 978-1-5262-0870-5

Printed in the United Kingdom.
First printing, 2021.

Rosa-Luxemburg-Stiftung London Office
c/o New Economics Foundation
10 Salamanca Place
SE17HB London, UK

www.global-gnd.com

CONTENTS

ACKNOWLEDGEMENTS

We are indebted to everyone that took the time to contribute to this publication, and also want to thank the people you collaborate with in your transformative work. Through it we can see a collective path to futures we need and deserve. Sean Sweeney (Trade Unions for Energy Democracy), Mika Minio-Paluello (Platform London and Transition Economics) and Tomaso Ferrando (Universiteit Antwerpen), thank you for your thoughtful recommendations.

Illustration by Molly Crabapple

1. CLIMATE JUSTICE IN A GLOBAL GREEN NEW DEAL

Harpreet Kaur Paul & Dalia Gebrial

If the Coronavirus pandemic provides an indication of our collective ability to cope with shocks, the future of the climate crisis does not look pretty. Take the case of India: on 24 March 2020 and with just four hours' notice, over 1.3 billion people found themselves in a Covid-19 spurred lockdown. As in many countries, those with access to savings or formal employment retreated to the safety of their homes. However, for a significant proportion of India's 40 million migrant labourers - many of whom live hand to mouth - lockdown left them stranded far away from home, without income. With road and rail networks closed and no resources to meet basic needs, many of those who keep society functioning - whether as domestic helpers, drivers, gardeners, street vendors, or as daily-wagers or construction workers - decided to walk hundreds of kilometres back to the villages they'd left behind, in some cases because of devastating climate impacts.[1] Many died en route.[2] Across the world, informal economy workers are disproportionately impacted by the crisis, with women particularly over-represented in precarious work.

---

1   Randall, Alex (2020). 'What does Covid-19 mean for people displaced by climate change?'. Le Monde Diplomatique.

2   Pandey, Geeta (2020). 'Coronavirus in India: Desperate migrant workers trapped in lockdown'. BBC News.

Within 'developed'[3] countries like the UK and US, we continue to see people of colour disproportionately impacted by the virus. Often living in densely populated, working-class neighbourhoods and working in highly exposed jobs like frontline care and transportation, black and brown people have found themselves on the frontline of Covid-19 impacts within countries most prepared for such shocks.[4] Those considered 'unproductive', such as the elderly and those with disabilities, have been sacrificed in service of an economy that sees them as burdens, rather than cherished members of our communities. Everywhere, police disproportionately enforced lockdown measures on those most impoverished and with least access to space.[5] The workers being put on the frontline are the same workers penalised for demanding protective equipment, and punished by increasingly hostile immigration policies and anti-migrant headlines. In other words: it is the most vulnerable and marginalised being left to pay the highest price during this global crisis.

Is it possible to learn from this painful preview? Can we instead re-organise how we work, care, move, rest and play to prioritise people and planet, especially in times of crisis? The need to re-shuffle and centre these needs

3   References to 'developed' and 'developing' follow UNFCCC definitions: UNFCCC. 'Parties & Observers'

4   Bristol Poverty Institute (2020). 'Poverty Dimensions of the Impact of Covid-19 on BAME communities'. University of Bristol.

5   Ratcliffe, Rebecca (2020). 'Teargas, beatings and bleach: the most extreme Covid-19 lockdown controls around the world'. The Guardian.

Illustration by Tomekah George

has long been the rallying cry of climate justice advocates across the world. Activists in the Global North have recently been re-energised by the Green New Deal framing to 'Build Back Better' from the climate crisis, creating green jobs, apprenticeships and re-training programmes to stimulate renewable energy generation, increase energy efficiency, reduce waste, promote sustainable transport and alter land use. Renationalising energy, waste, agriculture, and transport companies to carry this out efficiently, while also addressing fuel poverty with a combination of cheaper state generated clean energy and energy savings schemes (improving home insulation, for example) are important features.

Progressive Green New Deals look to tackle the climate crisis through a transformative political and economic programme. This means wide-scale investment in public infrastructure, the provision of free or cheap green transportation and reorienting away from oligarchal energy companies towards a democratic community or public ownership model. The Green New Deal framing also focuses on a just transition, ensuring that jobs lost in carbon intensive industries are transferred to decent work in the renewable energy and energy efficiency sectors, as well as reforestation or organic agro-ecology industries. These developments represent somewhat of a shift in climate thinking in the Global North, which had previously framed 'the environment' and climate action as abstract categories, separable from economic and political systems. Much of this shift is due to a long overdue lesson, learned from the holistic approaches of climate justice movements in the Global South and by Indigenous communities.

However, the Green New Deal has largely been trapped in national imaginations. Activists and politicians in North America and Europe have developed compelling visions for how such a programme could be transformative on a national scale - but the story of climate change is global and therefore its solutions, too, must be global. If Global North activists seek decarbonisation at a pace inconsistent with keeping warming below 1.5°C - that has a direct impact on those on the frontline

9

of seas rising, heat, water and food stress, disease spread and increasingly regular and strong storms, wildfires, droughts (often leading to long-term desertification), and floods. While record-breaking financing and state handouts for the fossil fuel intensive industries continues to abet rising emissions, the need to meet the Paris Agreement targets of keeping global temperature well below 2°C above pre-industrial levels has never been clearer.

The difference between the two Paris Agreement numbers is also stark. The difference in impacts between an increase of 1.5°C, and an increase of 2°C, in global average surface temperature is significant. In NASA's summary of the IPCC's October 2018 Special Report,[6] they state that an estimated 61 million more people would be exposed to severe drought due to lack of water availability at 2°C, in comparison to 1.5°C. 50% fewer people would see increased climate change-induced water stress at 1.5°C. Between 184-270 million fewer people are projected to be exposed to increases in water insecurity at 1.5°C. According to WWF, limiting temperature rises to 1.5°C would also result in 1.3 billion fewer people experiencing regular heatwaves, and 65 million fewer people exposed to exceptional heat waves.[7] 10 million fewer people would be exposed to sea level rise related loss and damage.

If we continue as we are, we will overreach the limits set out by the Paris Agreement. Exact estimates vary, but most see global average surface temperature rise reaching about 4°C by the end of this century. This will likely render much of the equatorial belt uninhabitable for much of the year, with Saharan deserts spreading into southern and central Europe. Two thirds of the glaciers that feed many of Asia's rivers will be lost. Existing policies would limit this warming to 2.8°C, but there is no court responsible for making states follow-through with their policies, and their pledges and targets are non-binding.

While ambitious decarbonisation is necessary, many of the demands being made in the North, such as around renewable transportation, will have significant impacts on supply chains and environmental sustainability around the world. Ushering green energy to the Global North and the expense of people in the majority Global South having access to their basic needs is antithetical to the notion of a Global Green New Deal. Neglecting the interdependent nature of both the climate crisis and responses to it risks creating

---

6 Buis, Alan (2019). 'A Degree of Concern: Why Global Temperatures Matter, Part 2.' NASA.

7 WWF (n.d). 'Half a degree matters.' WWF-UK.

a new era of 'green colonialism.' We cannot accept a model of 'progress' that relies on exploiting workers who mine the minerals and metals for renewable energy generation, or which allows for the continued concentration of land ownership and access in the hands of a few. We cannot replace our fossil fuel centred economy - where a country like Nigeria can derive 86% of its export revenue from oil and gas while two-thirds of the population live below the poverty line[8] - with green energy that maintains the same dynamics of who has access to what. To do so would be to miss the opportunity to not just build back, but build anew in the knowledge that another world is possible; a world where clean energy, food, water, housing, transport, care and health needs are universally met, without exception.

The way we understand and mobilise around the Green New Deal needs to change. This includes how we frame our movements, our policy proposals and our vision for change over the coming years. This means rooting calls for climate justice in global understandings of responsibility, accountability and reparation.

This book pools the knowledge of climate activists from around the world to offer an alternative frame for the Green New Deal - one that is rooted in principles of global justice, and understands the interdependent nature of the problem and its solution. It pushes beyond abstract platitudes of 'internationalism', instead using case studies of concrete policy and movement frameworks from around the world to inspire further action; to challenge those working under the Green New Deal framework to think beyond national borders. We reject the false and fanciful solutions put forward by political and financial elites, which merely continues an energy system based on extractivism and neocolonialism. Instead, this publication stands in the tradition of the 1991 multinational People of Color Environmental Leadership Summit's seventeen principles of Environmental Justice,[9] and the decades of climate justice leadership that has arisen from the majority Global South ever since.

The vision informing this publication is one that seeks to limit warming to 1.5°C above pre-industrial levels.[10] This vision also sees communities on the frontline of climate change receiving the resources they need to address the consequences of our already warmed world. It looks at pathways out of the

---

8 OPEC (2020). Nigeria: Facts and Figures. OPEC.

9 Alston, Dana (2010). 'The Summit: Transforming a Movement.' Reimagine: Race, Poverty and the Environment. .

10 IPCC (2018). 'Global Warming of 1.5°C: An IPCC Special Report.' IPCC.

climate crisis that are rooted in principles of democratic ownership, gender justice, anti-racism and anti-colonialism.

At the heart of this, is a reparative framework that places the responsibility on historic emitters in the Global North to take on their fair share of the struggle for a sustainable world. This means striving for zero carbon by 2030, scaling up climate financing, welcoming migrants, re-thinking land access, distribution and food justice, and providing the resources, know-how, and patents waivers for clean technology to countries that need it.

Frames alone cannot challenge increased mining by Rio Tinto in Australia or on elephant sanctuaries in India. They cannot push back against the global deepening of institutionalised and mandated austerity and privatisation, which take us further away from ensuring universal social protection. They cannot give countries the fiscal and policy space to prioritise people and planet, or stop the continued reliance on fossil fuels. They cannot overhaul extractivist trade agreements that enable the making of things by precarious workers in the majority Global South for the benefit of those of us in the minority Global North. They cannot increase our collective capacity to experience global pandemics, climate change, or economic recessions in a way that does not ask those least responsible to pay the greatest price. What we hope this frame can do, is propose a set of broad principles and red lines within which we can collectively operate and take action. It is up to those reading this publication to build the movements and policy action that will change our world for the better.

Our world at 1.1°C is already disproportionately hurting those least culpable. The wealthiest in the minority Global North have the greatest responsibility to repair these impacts and prevent future unmanageable warming. Current state pledges and climate action ambitions, if fulfilled, would still see around 2.8°C of global average surface temperature rise. As it stands, even these insufficient targets are unlikely to be met, as they rely on future carbon capture technologies that are at best impracticable and at worst will continue environmental racism through resource extraction and waste dumping. At the same time, resources to adapt to and repair the harmful effects of historic emissions already in motion are concealed from those most in need. Worse, available funds are too often redirected to those causing the problem through fossil fuel and agri-business subsidies while climate, humanitarian and development financing is squeezed.

The response to climate breakdown requires a global vision that addresses the root causes of how we got here. This publication aims to outline the drivers of the problems, and suggests how we can create the new world, where the needs of the many are not sacrificed for the profits and power of the few.

This publication is split into eight themes, which represent the key policy and movement planks of a Global Green New Deal: work; health, housing and social protection; trade and investment; land and food; water; the movement of people; foreign policy and debt and reparations. These themes were identified during workshops conducted as part of the 'Climate Justice' programming stream in The World Transformed Festival 2019.[11] Each theme is introduced by us and then moves to interventions from policy workers, activists and civil society organizations from around the world.

---

11 With thanks to Asad Rehman, Kate Arnoff, Jason Hickel, Jyoti Fernandes, Katie McKenna, Simon Pirani, Nathan Thanki, David Wearing, Rajiv Sicora, Mika Minio-Paluello, Minda Burgos-Lukes, Patrick O'Callaghan, and the many others who participated and assisted.

Illustration by Molly Crabapple

2. WORK IN A JUSTICE CENTERED TRANSITION

To stay below 1.5°C, industries like solar, wind and battery storage must expand rapidly, and fossil fuels must stay in the ground. Much has been written about the need to retrain workers in carbon intensive industries for a planned transition into decent green employment. This is particularly important in the Covid-19 era where thousands of people have lost employment just as the need for long-term job creation, resilience and sustainability to withstand health, climate and economic shocks becomes clearer. Transitions take time, resources and vision - but workers in fossil fuel intensive industries can be protected through pensions (for older workers) and funded retraining into guaranteed green work schemes for younger workers. Education providers must start offering courses to equip a new generation of engineers, construction workers, plumbers, metal workers, architects and others to be part of a low-carbon future. Work must always provide living wages, safe working conditions (workers producing solar panels, for example, deal with a number of toxic substances and electrical hazards),   and give workers a meaningful voice in decision-making, including through ensuring freedom of association. Workers cooperatives can create deeper worker democracy.

Public ownership and investment of a green stimulus could create millions of jobs in:

- Passive housing construction so that infrastructures generate more energy than they use through energy efficiency retrofits and embedded SMART renewable energy generation infrastructure;
- public transport upgrades and innovative electric car sharing schemes;
- ecological restoration and land, forestry, and agriculture improvements; and
- community energy, waste, and manufacturing infrastructure.

Such commitments are essential given that, globally, governments are planning to produce about 50% more fossil fuels in 2030 than would be consistent with limiting warming to 2°C and 120% more than would be consistent with limiting warming to 1.5°C.[1] Outputs from the fossil fuel industry continue to grow[2] with the benefit of government handouts (approximately USD$500 billion in 2019),[3] unprecedented support from private banks (global banks funneled USD$2.7 trillion into fossil fuels since Paris Climate Agreement)[4], and the confidence that they can expect business as usual without political shifts towards progressive Green New Deals. The need to protect workers from heat stress as temperatures rise above 51°c in India and Pakistan (for example) is also well documented, as is the need to create work for those on the frontline of climate change impacts.[5]

Furthermore, whilst the transition to renewable infrastructure (such as electric cars) often headlines Green New Deal discussions in the Global North, there is little acknowledgement of the exploitative assembly lines of these supposedly green goods, and the extractive mining of minerals and metals they require. Global production of batteries, solar panels, electric car motors, fuel cells, nuclear reactors and wind turbines relies on rare earth minerals and metals that are overwhelmingly sourced from the Global South, often under appalling ecological and labour conditions. With China dominating the man-

---

1   UN Environment Programme (2019). 'World's government plan to produce 120% more fossil fuels by 2030 than can be burned under 1.5°C warming.' UN.

2   Hausfather, Zeke (2018). 'Analysis: Fossil-fuel emissions in 2018 increasing at fastest rate for seven years.' CarbonBrief.

3   AFP (2020). '2019 fossil fuel subsidies nearly $500bn: OECD/IEA.' France24.

4   BankTrack et al., (2020). 'Banking on Climate Change: Fossil Fuel Finance Report 2020.' BankTrack

5   ILO Work Income and Equity Unit (2019). 'Working on a warming planet: The impact of heat stress on labour productivity and decent work.' ILO.

ufacturing of solar PV and lithium-ion batteries, what happens on the factory floors of Guangzhou should be as central to envisioning a Green New Deal as rebuilding industry in the rust-belt of the US or de-industrialised impoverished parts of rural Britain.

Communities at the frontline of the extraction of these minerals are experiencing displacement, internal and external conflict (including threats and killings of land defenders and movement leaders), eroded livelihoods, contaminated air, soil and water, lack of access to arable land and freshwater, economic dependence, severe health impacts, and cultural loss as peoples are severed from their land. At the manufacturing level, exploitative conditions with long hours, poverty wages, union busting, and health and safety concerns are endemic.

This is also a gendered issue. Women who work with toxic chemicals face reproductive health issues, while women engaging in unpaid sustenance farming or care work face heightened difficulties, particularly where they must travel further for access to clean water, undertake care for longer periods as younger generations migrate to urban areas unimpacted by saltwater intrusion, or have to cultivate on land in a context of desertification.[6]

A holistic Global Global Green New Deal would need to:
- repair historic gendered injustices, including with regards to paid and unpaid labour
- reduce consumption of renewable energy powered goods; promoting re-use, repair and mending, as well as sharing;
- seek international agreements and governance mechanisms to fairly allocate the supply of the available rare minerals and metals.

Trade agreements must ensure workers' rights protection and environmental sustainability standards that empower workers and communities to expand their negotiating power. They must facilitate worker and community-led green industrial strategies in mining and manufacturing areas and leverage public purchasing power by ensuring socially, environmentally and climate-responsible procurement that meets ILO and human rights frameworks, and democratises energy and mining companies complicit in supply chain horrors.

---

6 Any references to "women" or "womxn" in this publication refers to an inclusive definition, which welcomes trans women, genderqueer women, and non-binary people

No worker left behind
SEBASTIAN ORDOÑEZ MUÑOZ

Sebastian Ordoñez Muñoz is Senior International Programmes
Officer (Latin America) at War on Want, based in London,
UK.

The recent mainstreaming of the Green New Deal framework has intensified scrutiny on oil majors. However, the same cannot be said of global extractivist power - especially mining companies, who see the climate crisis as an opportunity to reinvent themselves and guarantee their bottom line. Supported by the World Bank,[7] the mining industry has cynically positioned itself as key actors in the energy transition, claiming they are needed to provide the minerals and metals to meet growing renewable energy demand.[8] Yet, many of these same companies are heavily invested in fossil fuel extractors, and are among the world's highest corporate emitters.[9]

The mining industry, along with other extractive industries, has been at the heart of a colonial model which continues to bring profits to multinational corporations and the wealthy few, while dispossessing countless communities of their lands, water and livelihoods and exploiting workers at the expense of their health and well-being.

Miners are also amongst the most mistreated workers in the world. In July 2019, at least 43 artisanal miners died in the Democratic Republic of the Congo (DRC), due to a mine collapse at an industrial copper and cobalt mine owned by Anglo-Swiss multinational Glencore (cobalt is a vital part of electric car batteries). UNICEF estimates that 40,000 children work in mining across the south of the DRC. Meanwhile, Glencore sees itself as part of the energy transition powering the electric vehicle revolution.During the pandemic, multiple governments declared

7   Hund et al., (2020). 'Minerals for Climate Action: The Mineral Intensity of the Clean Energy Transition.' World Bank Group.

8   Auciello, Benjamin Hitchcock (2019). 'A Just(ice) Transition is a Post-Extractive Transition.'

9   Oberle et al., (2019). 'Global Resources Outlook 2019: Natural resources for the future we want.' UN Environment.

mining an essential activity, or responded to industry pressure to do so after a brief shutdown. Mining operations became vectors of the disease -- for workers and rural communities. As companies profiteered from the pandemic, threats to land defenders exercising legitimate protest increased, and the regulatory groundwork was laid to reposition and bolster extractivist industries.

Mining and the 'green' recovery

The conversation in the North has turned to the need for a 'green' recovery: substantial stimulus packages to re-activate economic activity, doused in largely cosmetic green-growth commitments that do little to address the systemic nature of the climate crisis.

With many Southern economies forced to rely on resource extraction for income, falling demand and prices will not only further expose the vulnerabilities of their economies, but will cement the logic that increasing production of such resources is the sole tool for economic recovery. However, increasing the rate and scale of extraction will only result in huge environmental, social and health impacts for people and planet. [10]

For a long time, the global mining industry has tried to pit its workers against climate justice movements and communities on the frontlines of ecological collapse. Though historic tensions exist between environmental and labour politics that must be overcome, this fabricated dichotomy is made possible in part by the well-rehearsed maxim that mining brings economic development, which is heavily pushed by states and industry.

There is another way

The clamour to replace one extractive industry with another obscures the fact that the biggest factor in human impact on planetary ecology is economic growth. It also promotes the reliance on technology as the sole vehicle to reduce carbon emissions. While improvements in technology efficiency help reduce the material and energetic

10 Zarate, Camila (2020). 'Los impactos ambientales del Plan de Reactivacion Económica'. OLCA.

intensity of economic activity, these improvements have not succeeded in bringing about an absolute reduction in impact.

Transitioning our energy system must not come at the expense of workers. We need to correct the lack of effective and binding mechanisms to ensure the respect of human rights, with international legal norms that hold transnational corporations accountable for the abuses along their complex supply chains. Human rights treaties binding on corporations and their supply webs, ethical procurement, worker and community led decision making, can all play a role. As can innovation in energy storage, transmission, distribution, generation and supply techniques that do not rely on raw earth minerals and metals. Workers and communities should be able to ask, for whose benefit are the mines? Will they have equitable access to the resources mined and the final products - whether renewable energy or otherwise - made from the raw materials? Can the mines be closed and a fair allocation of energy still be maintained? In this case, social protection for mining workers and communities must be ensured.

Ultimately, the solutions are fundamentally social; technical fixes and increases in efficiency alone do not bring about justice or ecological well being. However, on the demand side, there are ways to enable us to make better-informed choices about our energy and resource consumption. Such changes should lead to reduced consumption and re-use, or widespread sharing of available materials, significantly lowering the need for new resource extraction. Communities and workers on the frontlines need the resources to articulate a new alternative to the dominant development model.

Justice and equity must touch every aspect of the transition, leaving no being behind. Increasing access to energy, food and public services goes hand-in-hand with reducing excess consumption through processes of redistribution that guarantee jobs and livelihoods. A truly Global Green New Deal[11] is an opportunity to put climate justice front and centre as the world enters a post-pandemic recession. However, this begins by ensuring that recovery or transition in the Global North does not happen at the further expense of ecological and worker well being in the Global South. ●

11 www.globalgnd.org

Womxn's work and the just transition
KAVITA NAIDU

Kavita Naidu was, until recently, Climate Justice Programme Officer at Asia Pacific Forum On Women, Law And Development, based in Chiang Mai, Thailand.

Since the financial crisis of 2008, the political left in the US and UK have been advocating for a Green New Deal[12] as the transformational socio-economic response to tackle the climate crisis. So far, all GNDs - whether national or international - aim to dismantle the profit-driven fossil fuel economy, and transition equitably to a 'green economy' that promotes social, gender and economic justice.

The feasibility of the Green New Deal[13] depends on whether it reflects the scale of the challenges faced in the Global South as a result of extraction and exploitation of natural resources, energy and cheap labour by the developed North.[14] Imperial trade liberalization has saddled the Global South with alarming debt. High interest rates compounded by structural adjustment policies have paralysed the ability of Southern states to invest in public infrastructure, build environmental resilience, tackle health crises like Covid-19 - let alone fund a GND.

Womxn of the Global South bear the brunt of the insecurity and work generated by these policies. Trade rules dictating the privatisation of essential services[15] in healthcare, sanitation, water and education have disproportionately burdened womxn, who take on the gendered, unpaid work of collecting water and fuel, cleaning, preparing food and providing care for children, the elderly and ill. Over 75% of unpaid care work in the world is undertaken by poor womxn and girls who can spend up to 14 hours a day doing care work in rural areas. Their contribution to the global economy when valued at minimum wage is $10.8

12 Dauncey, Guy (2019). 'Ten Green New Deals - How Do They Compare.'

13 Kolinjivadi, Vijay (2019). 'Why a 'Green New Deal' must be decolonial.' Al Jazeera.

14 McQuade, Joseph (2019). 'Earth Day: Colonialism's role in the overexploitation of natural resources.' The Conversation.

15 Khan, Tessa and Marion Sharples (2017). GADN Briefings: Making trade work for gender equality. Gender & Development Network.

trillion[16] - more than three times the value of the global tech industry. In developing countries, 90% of women are working in the informal sector[17], and their unpaid domestic work subsidizes the capitalist economy. In other words, wealth for the rich is accumulated by eradicating basic labor and human rights of womxn and girls across the world.[18]

Neo-liberalism demands gendered divisions of labour that place the burden of precarity on womxn. Meanwhile, these same womxn are left to face insufferable pollution[19], displacement[20] and dispossession[21] in the name of profit and economic growth. Despite contributing the least to the climate crisis, womxn of the Global South bear the brunt of unpredictable seasonal patterns[22] that destroy their crops and water sources, harm health, cripple food sovereignty, force greater poverty, and expose them to violence and conflict, entrapping womxn in a cycle of intergenerational inequality and discrimination.

Given this context, how can a GND reverse the dominant economic system, which persistently undervalues, invisibilises and exploits Southern womxn's labour to sustain 'growth' in the North?

Without shifting from the rhetoric of 'growth' and addressing the historical and gendered injustices that have caused climate, ecological and health crises, the GND risks reinforcing 'business-as-usual' - promoting 'green' colonialism masked as 'sustainable development'.[23]

A feminist and human-rights based 'decolonial' GND must overhaul technocratic and market driven solutions that merely "cost shift"[24] to more marginalized populations - especially womxn. It must center the social well being of the most vulnerable by redistributing capital and resources in the form of climate reparations and binding Common But

16 Oxfam (n.d.). 'Not all gaps are created equal: the true value of care work.' Oxfam International.

17 Schalatek, Liane (2020). 'The invisible coronavirus makes systemic gender inequalities and injustices visible.' Heinrich Böll Stiftung.

18 Elliot, Larry (2019). 'World's 26 richest people own as much as poorest 50%, says Oxfam.' The Guardian.

19 WECAN (n.d.). 'Why women.' WECAN International.

20 Sarkar, Soumya (2020). 'Women suffer the most from climate displacement.' India Climate Dialogue.

21 Löw, Christine (2020). 'Under cover of the pandemic, stealth land grabs are ongoing.' OpenDemocracy.

22 UN Human Rights Council (2019). 'Analytical study on gender-responsive climate action for the full and effective enjoyment of the rights of women.' UN

23 Gebrial, Dalia (2019). 'As the left wakes up to climate injustice, we must not fall into 'green colonialism''. The Guardian.

24 Kolinjivadi, Vijay and Ashish Kothari (2020). 'No Harm Here is Still Harm There: The Green New Deal and the Global South (II).' Jamhoor.

Differentiated Responsibility (CBDR).[25] Resources should be mobilised to secure vast public financing of essential and environmentally viable public infrastructure. Fossil fuel subsidies must cease and budgets from military and prison industrial complexes redirected to developing social protection schemes, decent work, redistributing care, ecological regeneration and restoration - lifting the burden of unpaid care and domestic work from the shoulders of marginalised women.

A Global Green New Deal must shape a new social contract that re-orients this broken economic system away from unrestrained exploitation of natural resources and labour to one built on human dignity, solidarity, equity and protecting our planet. ●

Fighting for good, green jobs in the wake of Covid-19
VICENTE P. UNAY

Vicente P. Unay, Jr. is Secretary General at National Union Of Workers In The Power Industry (Power-Sentro), based in Quezon City, Philippines.

→   *The just transition from oil and gas jobs to decent jobs in the renewable sector has been thrown into uncertainty by the Covid-19 pandemic. The crisis has not only exposed the deficiencies of a market-oriented healthcare system that treats health as a commodity, but also the situation of precarious workers and income inequality. Overseas Filipino workers from different parts of the world were transported back to the country - and those in the transport and informal labour sectors suffered loss of income due to lockdown and enhanced community quarantine for 3 months. Under the pretext of the pandemic, the Department of Labour and Employment (DOLE)*

25 Climate Nexus (n.d.) 'Common but differentiated responsibilities and Respective Capabilities (CBDR-RC).

advisory allowed employers and employees to negotiate adjustments in their contract - such as reduction in work hours, compressed work week and increased flexible working arrangement. Workers who were laid off were unable to file a case as quasi-judicial bodies of DOLE were suspended, and had limited information, procedure and access for filing an online complaint.

To sum up, nearly 10 million workers were unprotected in a time of crisis, and lost their job.

It does not have to be like this. Crises like the pandemic and climate change can be an opportunity for the working classes to build towards social transformation; a shift where the preservation of human life and sustainable environment is the centre of development.

The labour movement[26] in the Philippines is united in fighting the pandemic, climate change and the creeping authoritarian regime. For SENTRO, which represents 80,000 workers across different sectors, this must involve rapidly building up the country's public health system, in order to protect from the health impacts of the continued denudation of the environment, climate change and future pandemics. It also means seeing this as a chance to alter income inequality in the country by introducing an income guarantee - a prelude to universal income. With the government being forced to bail out corporations, now is the time for the labour movement to press for changes in the power balance underpinning industrial relations.

However, the trade union movement is constrained by legislation such as the 2012 Cybercrime Prevention Act, the 2020 Anti-Terrorism law and the 2020 BAHO Act (which gave the President additional powers to fight Covid-19). These laws are designed by the Duterte administration to sow public fear, legitimise human rights violations and undermine democracy and freedom of the press. SENTRO therefore sees the fight against climate change, labour rights violations, looming dictatorship and the recent pandemic as interrelated.

The Philippines are one of the lowest CO_2 emitting countries in the world. Yet, as an archipelagic island situated between the Pacific Ocean and South China Sea, it is frequently affected by extreme

---

26 SENTRO, Nagkaisa (the biggest broad labour coalition in the Philippines) and other broad civil society organizations.

weather events, like typhoons. When typhoons hit, the transmission lines and electric distribution posts are heavily devastated, and take 3-6 months to rehabilitate - a period that hampers provincial economies.

Yet, the current energy supply remains heavily dependent on coal as its primary source for power generation.[27] The long-term Philippine Energy Plan (PEP) has been criticised for its "lack of focus" on clean energy,[28] especially as the Shell-operated Malampaya gas field is expected to be exhausted within the next 4 to 5 years.

SENTRO has been mobilizing with other movements to put the Philippines on the path to clean energy. This includes mobilizing against coal power plants with the Philippine Movement for Climate Justice, working with ATM - an alliance to stop mining - to end extractive and open pit mining, and as a petitioner in Greenpeace Philippines' public case against carbon polluters like Chevron, Caltex and Shell.

SENTRO is also resisting the corporatization of electric cooperatives. For forty years, publicly funded electric cooperatives have provided electricity to 13 million household consumer-members, including rural areas.[29] The privatisation of these cooperatives means higher electricity bills for consumers (the highest in Asia), frequent blackouts, unstable supply and many still without power. For workers, it means cutting jobs and increasing reliance on contracted labour with lower wages and no benefits.[30]

In 2013, San Miguel Energy Corporation privatized the Albay Electric Cooperative (ALECO), after five years of workers resistance. High rates and inefficient services led many in the community to refuse paying their bills. The company disconnected the electric services of consumer-members who, in solidarity with striking workers, boycotted the payment of the electricity bill. On the other hand, the striking workers reconnected the electric service of disconnected community members. With unstable access to electricity, SENTRO introduced pilot renewable energy areas, and concluded a collective bargaining agreement that

27 Bunye, Patricia (2020). 'Energy 2020: Philippines.' Global Legal Insights.

28 Rivera, Danessa (2020). 'Fitch flags Philippines lack of focus on clean energy.' Philstar Global.

29 Union Aid Abroad - APHEDA (2018). 'Building union power through clean energy in the Philippines.' Union Aid Abroad - APHEDA.

30 PSI Comms (2018). 'Building workers' power in the utilities sector in Asia Pacific.' Public Services International.

created a Climate Justice and Just Transition Council.[31] However, at present, 9 electric cooperatives are under threat due to a corporate franchise grabbing bill, which is pending in Congress.

As long as the privatization of the power industry is permitted, attempts to decarbonise will only sustain business as usual - the transition to renewable energy and green jobs will be controlled by market-oriented policies, which hurts workers and their communities. Hence, the challenge for the trade union movement is to resist, reclaim and restructure the power industry towards energy democracy. That means public control and democratic governance of the power industry. Building a united global trade union movement is a must if we are to alter the power relations and change course away from false solutions to climate change. ●

Building workers' movements against false solutions
DANIEL GAIO

Daniel Machado Gaio is National Secretary Of Environment at Central Única Dos Trabalhadores (Cut), based in São Paulo, Brazil. Translated by Michael Fox.

Humanity's challenges have become more urgent since the beginning of Covid-19. In recent decades, the labor movement together with social movements and environmental organizations have denounced the unsustainability of the neoliberal model that created a health, social, ecological and climate crisis We have been pointing out alternative paths to this model - and now, they are even more urgent.

We find ourselves in a moment of a systematic dispute in which old answers disguised as sustainable will be highlighted as ways out of the

---

31 Mata, Joshua (2015). 'A social uprising for energy democracy.' New Internationalist.

Illustration by Tomekah George

crisis. False solutions masquerading as a 'green economy' will likely appear with substantial strength at a time when the world is demanding a different way out.

One sector that has invested heavily in false solutions is mining. Automation, IT and labor subcontracting are being presented to shareholders as the answer to the irresponsible and murderous reality of these companies' performance in the face of impacted communities, workers and biodiversity. Together, the ruptures of Vale dams in Bento Rodrigues[32] (2015) and Brumadinho[33] (2019) dumped 75 million liters of toxic tailings

32 Phillips, Dom (2015). 'Brazil's mining tragedy: was it a preventable disaster?'. The Guardian.

33 Phillips, Dom (2019). 'Brazilian mining company to pay out £86m for disaster that killed almost 300 people'. The Guardian.

mud, devastating entire communities, generating irrecoverable environmental losses, and claiming the lives of 278 people and 12 missing, mostly workers. To this day, families seek justice and reparations for the crime.

Meanwhile, in its institutional marketing, the company says that "it will invest at least USD$2 billion to reduce the company's carbon emissions by 33% by 2030. The biggest investment ever committed by the mining industry to fight climate change."[34] It's a transition that's not at all just.

This sector, together with agriculture and cattle ranching, has been responsible for deforestation, conflicts and contamination in the Amazon that have recently intensified. Retaining the same agricultural and mining systems, but without workers, is being presented as the answer to this crisis. This way, while production increases, jobs decrease and communities are threatened and harassed.

That's why unions and social movements are working towards the approval of a binding treaty that holds companies accountable and responds to those impacted in cases of environmental crimes and human rights violations. An effective transition cannot allow arrangements where companies self-present as sustainable while destroying the environment, exploiting and costing workers their lives.

In light of the scale of this challenge, we have been working intensively for these transformations to be made through global pacts, both in official spaces for climate negotiations at the UN and in our international alliances. These transformations must occur through the convergence between counter-hegemonic groups that bring proposals from workers, women, Blacks, Indigenous peoples and communities.

Beyond the challenges that deal with the old and new forms of work and precariousness, it is up to the labor movement to incorporate feminist and anti-racist eco-socialism as an aid in the fight over the model of development. Together, we can break away from this failed model, and build towards a system that focuses on life, employment and democracy. ●

---

34 WBCSD Communications (2020). 'Vale advances on the climate agenda and unveils US$D2 billion to reduce carbon emissions within the next ten years.' WBCSD.

Illustration by Molly Crabapple

3. LIVING WELL THROUGH SHOCKS: HEALTH, HOUSING AND SOCIAL PROTECTION

Climate change threatens our right to have a clean and safe environment in which to live. Increasingly strong storms, floods and wildfires cause loss of life and livelihood, and existing mechanisms to deal with this heightened risk are not only insufficient, but exclusionary. Often, marginalised communities will not have been consulted in the design of early warning systems and evacuation systems, causing particular risks to those who may need enhanced support.

The rights to live in dignity, with suitable access to housing, safe energy, a clean and safe environment, sustenance, and physical and mental health have been under threat for a long time. They have their roots in colonialism, which created a profound global cultural shift in how humans relate to nature and one another. It imposed a view that if we weren't always dominating and exploiting natural resources and other people, we weren't being 'productive'.

This directly conflicts with the beliefs of many indigenous peoples, for whom the relationship between people and nature is one of interdependence and stewardship, rather than domination and extraction. The systematic destruction of such principles has left swathes of the global population without adequate resources to prioritise the health and well-being of themselves, their family and community - meanwhile, wealth continues to accumulate for a small minority. The destruction of nature for extraction, industrial agriculture, urbanisation or industry development is also causing severe health crises. Zika, AIDS, SARS and Ebola all originated from animal populations under severe environmental pressures.[1]

Scientific developments in technology and medicine have enriched industries such as pharmaceuticals and agriculture. Yet, life saving drugs have become out of reach for many who are excluded from the rudimentary infrastructures for survival - basic social infrastructures like a comprehensive, accessible healthcare system and stable, safe housing. Neoliberal governance (which has pushed austerity measures within Global North countries and structural adjustment and privatisation in the South) have concentrated wealth for the few, while pushing millions into poverty. With climate breakdown comes the urgent need to reverse this course, and focus instead on building strong infrastructures of social protection and resilience - especially for communities most at risk.

Guppi Bola (Public health, climate justice, and decolonising economics expert) adds:

> *As the pandemic has demonstrated, health crises distribute themselves unevenly across the globe by following the patterns of existing structural marginalization. The health gap exists because these outcomes of ill-health are both avoidable and unfair. It is ultimately a result of political choices around investment of public resources, exposure to environmental pollution and other (including climate change linked) hazards, and access to stable decent and green employment with appropriate protective equipment. Health outcomes are complicated by biological weathering (the susceptibility of ill health due to ongoing trauma) which is slowly being recognised as a driver of health*

---

1   Carrington, Damian (2020). 'Pandemics result from destruction of nature, say UN and WHO.' The Guardian.

> *inequalities alongside barriers to accessing vital public health services, clean air and water, nutritious food, and sustainable work consistent with International Labour Organisation convention, human rights, and occupational health and safety standards.*

Across the world, the gap between the amount of affordable housing available, and the number of people who need it is increasing. By 2025, this gap is forecast to affect over a third of the world's urban population[2] - for 1.6 billion people around the world, this would mean living in unsafe and over-crowded high rises, in informal slums or sleeping rough. Extreme weather events cause disproportionate losses for vulnerable dwellers and those forced to live in informal settlements where women, young people, LGBTQI+, people who live with disabilities and older people face heightened risks of violence. One single storm can displace thousands of people, and cause a scale of property destruction that takes decades to recover from. In 2005, Hurricane Katrina destroyed 800,000 housing units in New Orleans. In 2019, Cyclone Idai is estimated to have destroyed 90% of Beira, a city of more than half a million people in Mozambique. Mozambique is the sixth poorest country in the world, and highly indebted - yet its coal and titanium mines and agro-industry has enriched investors around the world. Meanwhile, the people of Mozambique have suffered as a result of this economic model, facing reduced social security spending as the government seeks to repay its debts (especially in a climate of reduced income from its export commodities). In this neoliberal policy space, housing and other poverty alleviation efforts are systematically deprioritised over (foreign) investor friendly schemes that have concentrated wealth in the hands of a few.[3]

Black Lives Matter UK organiser and University of Warwick PhD candidate, Alexandra Wanjiku Kelbert, notes:

> *Storms and pandemics themselves cannot easily be averted. But the scale of the destruction wrought, and whether or not an event becomes a disaster or a catastrophe, is based on both the political decisions made in responding to a crisis and the history of decisions*

2   Woetzel et al. (2014). 'Tackling the world's affordable housing challenge.' McKinsey Global Institute.

3   Jubilee Debt Campaign (2020). 'Mozambique: Secret loans and unjust debts.' Jubilee Debt Campaign.

> *(entrenched in ideological priorities in favour of gentrification, foreign direct investment or loans over lifting local people and local solutions) that create the context in which an event takes place. Covid-19 has shown what many of us have known for a long time. Economically marginalised people of colour disproportionately exposed to higher levels of air pollution, poor housing conditions, healthcare deprivation or discrimination, and frontline or precarious work will be disproportionately impacted by shocks, whether health, climate or economic. This is true in the UK[4] as much as for the billions living in poverty in the Global South. If the pandemic is a portal (as Arundhati Roy suggests)[5], it should be a portal to the kind of world many of us have been working towards for generations, in our housing and land struggles, in our strikes and in our protests.*

A globally just Green New Deal must therefore include a vision of affordable, secure and dignified housing - built to protect people from the impacts of climate change that are already underway - in addition to decent work and social protection throughout everyone's life course. Social protection includes universal access to health and social care - systems whose existing lack of resilience in times of crisis has been highlighted by the Covid-19 pandemic.

Decades of allowing private companies to treat people's health as a business opportunity while defunding public healthcare infrastructure has created a two-tier global health system. While some can rely on cutting edge medical technology and expertise, many are left unable to access even a hospital bed. This inequalities wrought by this system will become exacerbated by climate breakdown. Indeed, there is a deep connection between climate and wellbeing - for one, climate change increases the likelihood and severity of future pandemics.[6] The intensification of heatwaves from France to Pakistan disproportionately impacts elderly people and those with pre-existing heart and lung conditions. Climate change also proliferates vector-borne diseases (such as dengue, yellow fever, zika, and malaria), and increases premature air pollution related deaths. Food and water scarcity create health consequences

---

4 Hirsh, Sophie (2020). 'This is why Covid-19 is disproportionately hurting people of colour.' GreenMatters.

5 Roy, Arundhati (2020). 'The pandemic is a portal.' Financial Times.

6 Lustgarten, Abraham (2020). 'How climate change is contributing to skyrocketing rates of infectious disease.' ProPublica.

linked to malnutrition. Wildfires impact breathing. In short, climate change is the number one threat to public health this century.[7] As a result the need for a resilient and universally accessible healthcare infrastructure and services is urgent now more than ever.

A Global Green New Deal needs to nurture a twenty-first century commons in place of an economy based on privatising humanity's basic needs. This includes building a society that promotes life-long learning, care, health, art, movement and music as part of overall well-being inspired by Buen Vivir[8] - the social philosophy inspiring movements in South America to work towards less consumption, and encourage cooperation within communities to fairly distribute available resources, rather than permit permanent accumulation by the wealthy. The alternative to this model of unsustainable growth at the top and scarcity at the bottom, can be one of rich abundance for the many.

The socially created asymmetries of climate change impacts
LEON SEALEY-HUGGINS

Dr. Leon Sealey-Huggins is Assistant Professor And Activist at University Of Warwick And Wretched Of The Earth Collective, based in Birmingham, UK.

> *The unfolding of climate breakdown is not an inevitable impact of geophysical and meteorological processes - although it does of course entail unprecedented geophysical effects. Rather, climate breakdown is harmful precisely because it magnifies existing health, economy, gender, age and other marginalising relations.*
>
> *To take an example, we might consider the plight of the Caribbean region. Despite being one of the lowest emitting parts of the world, the region is particularly prone to extreme weather events as a result of*

---

7 Watts et al. (2018). 'The 2018 report of the Lancet countdown on health and climate change: shaping the health of nations for centuries to come.' The Lancet 392(10163).

8 Balch, Oliver (2013). 'Buen vivir: the social philosophy inspiring movements in South America.' The Guardian.

climate change - and is not being supported to build climate resilient infrastructure for its people.

In 2017, the unprecedented Hurricane Irma hit the British Virgin Islands (BVI) with devastating force. However, compare the capacities of common Virgin Islanders to cope when the hurricane hit, versus those of the Islands' most famous occupant, 'Sir' Richard Branson. While thousands were forced to seek safety on neighbouring islands, unsure if their houses would remain standing once the storm passed and they returned, Branson hunkered down in his concrete bunker sipping wine.[9] Meanwhile, thousands of buildings were destroyed, costing billions of dollars, and at least four people lost their lives in the immediate impact - and more dying in the months that followed. The inequality embedded in peoples' ability to be protected by climate-related disasters already underway is not inevitable: it is a symptom of a housing system that does not respond to the majority of peoples' actual needs. There is no such thing as a 'natural' disaster. Rather, disasters are socially

9 Zhang, Benjamin (2017). 'Richard Branson is having a big sleepover party on his private island as Hurricane Irma approaches.' Business Insider.

Illustrations: Finnekah George

produced by uneven access to resources, and are compounded by inattention to the harms of particular socio-ecological relations.

Imagine, instead, if Branson's hoarded wealth was put to better use, in the form of a redistributive and reparative process that would have better protected all inhabitants of the BVI? If distributed reasonably, humanely and fairly, Branson's wealth would have easily covered the costs of retrofitting the entire building stock of the BVI, and probably a greater part of the wider Caribbean region. These buildings could be made to withstand the kinds of weather events we are likely to see on an almost annual basis. Moreover, if we turned our attention to other billionaires, like Amazon CEO Jeff Bezos, we could ensure the entire world's population have access to basic material and social needs,[10] in spite of disruption to supply chains caused by climate breakdown. Instead, during our global pandemic, the wealthiest have increased their proportion of wealth. US billionaires alone got $434 billion richer during the pandemic.[11] At the same time, the majority of people look to survive with increased (unpaid) care responsibilities and small handouts in the form of short-term and insufficient rent freezes, limited water and utility bill suspensions or occasional wage contributions.

While necessary, one-off redistribution of wealth would not be sufficient to resolve the ongoing structural processes that cause weather-related disasters. What is required is a long-term reorganisation of social relations and social priorities in a way that eliminates the role of the billionaire hoarders and uplift all communities in their wake. To do this requires liberatory community strength building which will no doubt take many forms, but the seeds of which are visible in many struggles globally, such as in the case of the community permaculture of farmers of Puerto Rico who are able to feed fellow community members in the wake of Hurricane Maria that struck the same season as Irma;[12] or in the experimental models of community building seen in Cooperation Jackson.[13] A Global Green New Deal that could scale these kinds of programmes offers the promise of a world where everyone has

10 Oxfam (2019). 'Billionaire fortunes grew by $2.5 billion a day last year as poorest saw their wealth fall.' Oxfam.

11 Frank, Robert (2020). 'American billionaires got $434 billion richer during the pandemic.' CNBC.

12 Liguori, Steph (2020). 'The Rebirth of a Puerto Rican Permaculture Farm.' The Culture-ist.

13 Cooperation Jackson (n.d.). 'Sustainable Communities Initiative.' Cooperation Jackson.

> *access to energy, health services, education, housing and local/organic food and where communities are also active agents in the decision making that governs their lives.* ●

When the World Health Organisation declared Covid-19 a global pandemic in March 2020, it meant understanding that no one is safe unless everyone is safe. This requires a radical rethinking about what our economies are for, what purpose are they supposed to fulfill if it's not to enable our collective safety and flourishing? Rather than continuing an economic model that depletes our environment, concentrates wealth, and subsidies carbon intensive industries, Emiliar Reyes outlines how universal access to housing and health - in addition to other forms of social protection - may be ensured. This is particularly important in the context of climate change as extreme weather events rip away homes, savings and resilience, salt water slowly creeps onto farm lands and rising temperatures desertify previously abundant subsistence lots, making them unharvestable. Some countries, such as India, Ethiopia and Mexico, are implementing work schemes to help communities on the frontline of climate change impacts secure income through green or other guaranteed work during climate shocks, including work to improve irrigation schemes, flood prevention measures, soil stabilization, reforestation works, rural transport maintenance and improved land tenure to increase climate change resilience. Future schemes could add training and employment opportunities in renewable energy generation, distribution and supply, energy efficiency (in manufacturing, transportation, building construction and operations) measures, organic agriculture and public transport provision.

A human rights centred approach to social protection would require that these schemes build long-term and sustainable opportunities that meet International Labour Organisation decent work standards. Only decent, green, and long-term guaranteed work can help communities save to increase their resilience to withstand inevitable climate change shocks. Short term work that does not offer sufficient workers' rights protection, training opportunities and sustainable work would be insufficient. In addition, a holistic approach to social protection requires dignity for all - not just those able to undertake formalised paid work - to be ensured through social security, whether cash transfers to those undertaking unpaid care work, working in informal precarious jobs, or those unable to work, asset building and community development to increase adaptive capacity to withstand climate change impacts and repair long standing marginalizations, social health protection (including maternal health), child and family schemes, disability and sickness welfare protections, pensions and clean green energy subsidies for those who need it to heat their homes and feed their families.

A decolonial, feminist Global Green New Deal for our 2020 challenges
EMILIA REYES

Emilia Reyes works for Equidad De Género: Ciudadanía, Trabajo Y Familia (Gender Equity: Citizenship, Work And Family), based in Mexico City.

Multilateralism is in crisis, prioritizing profit over wellbeing. Over the years, financing conditionalities imposed by the IMF and the World Bank have required fiscal austerity, trade liberalisation, deregulation and privatisation of social and economic sectors. This has exacerbated developing countries' vulnerability to health epidemics, social, environmental and economic shocks, as well as climate change. The Bretton Woods institutions, the OECD and the UN have encouraged increased reliance on (unaccountable) private financing for development and humanitarian responses.[14] The Women's Working Group on Financing for Development (WWG on FfD)[15], now more than ever, sees the need for a comprehensive and systemic response while promoting a democratic transformation of how global governance takes place.

A decolonial feminist Global Green New Deal must upend the structures that deplete wealth, resources, nature in the Global South

14 Kentikelenis et al., (2020). 'Softening the blow of the pandemic: will the International Monetary Fund and the World Bank make things worse?'. The Lancet 8(6).

15 The WWG on FFD is an alliance of women's organizations and networks to advocate for the advancement of gender equality, women's empowerment and human rights in the Financing for Development related UN processes. It's currently co-convened by the Feminist Task Force and Equidad de Genero: Ciudadania, Trabajo y Familia.

to fuel consumption for the most wealthy, and an economy that relies on unpaid domestic and care work from women or pays marginalised women precariously to undertake this labour.

We join the Civil Society Financing for Development call to challenge existing economic, trade and financial dynamics. Under the umbrella of a call for a UN Economic Reconstruction and Systemic Reform Summit, we want to work towards a New Global Economic Architecture[16] that works for people and planet.

We must bring redistributive justice and environmental integrity to the center. We are continuing to erode public spending, especially in relation to crucial life giving and making sectors such as health and education at the very time we should be learning why care work, adaptive infrastructures and expansive universal social protection (maternal health, child, social and health care, life-long education and decent work, and pensions, for example) that protects everyone throughout our life course are absolutely vital. Only by ensuring this - as we undergo decarbonization processes - can we ensure a justice centred transition. New Green Deals must include these decolonial and feminist approaches, especially as we witness the attacks on indigenous peoples (who now make up less than 5% of the world's population, but preserve 80% of the planet's biodiversity)[17], local communities, and those facing multidimensional discrimination on the basis of the lottery of our geography, exposure to poverty, gender and gender identity, sexuality, age, indigenous or minority status and disability, national or social origin, birth or other status.

This means rejecting false solutions based in the financialization of development that rely on private exploitation of what should be recognized as commons. This also means centring redistributive justice in our understanding of what an economy is for and how it functions. We can do this with progressive taxation (so that those who can afford to contribute to the well-being of all), ending subsidies for carbon intensive industries (fossil fuel, construction, agroindustry, mining, and arms industries, for example), tackling illicit financial flows, and committing to

---

16 CS FFD Group (2020). 'Time for a UN Economic Reconstruction and Systemic Reform Summit.' Civil Society Financing for Development Group.

17 UN (2019). 'UN Report: Nature's Dangerous Decline 'Unprecedented'; Species Extinction Rates 'Accelerating.' UN.

running economies for people and the future of our planet.

We must give fiscal sovereignty to developing countries to decide which social protection regulations are in their interest, and hold them to account to deliver these. We must give fiscal space through debt cancellation and tax justice, place a moratorium on unfair trade and investment agreements (especially on vaccines, medical treatments and technology, as well as on food systems), and regulate financial institutions and markets. We believe this is the time to form alliances amongst social movements to ensure humanity finds its path again towards justice and wellbeing for people and planet. The time to act is now. ●

In any state organised social protection for development, climate policy or humanitarian responses, the voices of those on the frontline are essential. Alternatives are possible, and in the piece below Jale Samuwai outlines examples from Fiji.

Doing development differently
JALE SAMUWAI

Dr. Jale Simuwai is Climate Finance Advisor at Oxfam in the
Pacific, based in Suva, Fiji Islands.

Covid-19 for all its devastating health, economic and social impacts, has provided us with a unique opportunity to reflect on how we engage with climate change questions and development in general. Climate change as re-affirmed by Covid-19 is not merely an environmental problem, it is the consequence of a flawed development system that we have considered normal for too long. The conversations on climate change and Covid-19 are therefore not distinct, but are at their core a conversation about development itself.

Development as eloquently put by Dr. Tacisius Tabukaulaka – is a set of ideas that creates an image of what we want to become. The prevalent ideas that currently drive our development thinking are grounded in neoliberal economic ideologies. For Fiji and the majority of the Pacific countries, our development system is part of our colonial heritage, and this is evident in the extractive economic policies that have historically driven our development. Our existing development system promotes capitalistic thinking that sidelines the wellbeing of communities and the environment, and prioritises the need of big corporations and large-scale extraction of natural resources as the ideal pathway for achieving a better future for all. It is an established ideology that also promotes cut throat competition, rewards and incentivises individualism rather than the cordial and mutual cooperation of all. At the core of this development thinking is an extractive ideology that promotes and sustains the interest of the privileged few rather than those who have little.

There is a growing yearning from communities for real change on how the development system in our country operates. This means shifting our governance structures and decision making processes, and pushing for bold, fearless political leadership that is committed to a radical overhaul of institutions that are meant to be for the public good. Fiji made unpopular but necessary decisions that defied neoliberal logic to protect the safety and wellbeing of our people during the Coronavirus crisis. Despite the economic impacts, Fiji implemented a lockdown immediately upon its first recorded Covid-19 case, forbidding travel within cities as well as inter-island travel. This had severe economic implications especially for local businesses, and even though we have no community cases, curfew is still imposed from 11pm till 4am is still enforced nationwide. Now the same level of courage must be shown in the long and difficult decisions required to tackle climate change. We need leaders to move away from viewing everything from an economic perspective, and make development decisions because it is the right thing to do for holistic human and planetary well-being. They must have the courage to say no to lucrative development opportunities such as those in the extractive industries, and ask - for who are they lucrative? They must champion only the projects that place the well-being of all Fijans and the environment at its core.

This requires radical inclusion. Fiji needs to re-evaluate how it has been framing its development questions when it comes to whose voices we listen to, who should be sitting at the decision table and crucially, who is missing from critical decisions that influence the quality of life for all our citizens. This is essential in holding our states to account to re-prioritise widespread well-being over short-term investment which is anyway soon to be extracted and exported abroad.

Right now, in critical forums that determine general well-being, it is the rural remote women, the persons with disabilities, indigenous people, young people, LGBTQI communities and faith-based organizations that are always missing - whose voices are either muted or distorted. It is high time we stop talking about people who experience vulnerability and the marginalisation in societies, and instead listen to them.

When we bring those voices that have been devalued and sidelined for so long into the core of our development solution formulation, new and profound solutions for our development problems, including that of climate change, will begin to surface. Fiji, I believe, doesn't need big ideas to solve most of our obvious development problems - what we need is the insight and priorities from the practical experiences of our local people being valued, heard and acted upon.

Covid-19 has shown us that ultimately, our safety net is our community. Our ability to be resilient in the face of great uncertainties lies in our relationships with each other and our values. There is an urgent need for us as Fijians to relearn our local and indigenous values and principles and for these to be embedded in the core of our development and education systems.

A famous itaukei idiom resonates for me here: "ni dau loveci ga na kau ni se gone"- meaning you can only change people's behaviour and thinking when they are young. Building an education system for young people that does not follow the neoliberal model of promoting competition, individualism, consumerism and materialistic wealth is key to shifting the system towards a fair future for all - in a way that is sustainable and long term. ●

Communities are often our safety but they have faced decades of erosion. A key obstacle to financing social protections schemes that uphold community well-being in countries within the Global South is the significant debt burden they face, and the constant drive for growth driven by international development institutions. Whether it's forests in Bhutan or ocean creatures in a blue economy, everything is seen as having the potential to grow GDPs in a way that is compatible with sustainable futures. At the same time, governments in the Global South spend more and more on debt repayments, curtailing education and health. Often, reduced public spending is a requirement of loans of development projects. Reduced social services have a particular impact on women who support education, care and health related work.

Such measures concentrate wealth among a small minority while the majority have less but work more. The ability to live a good life is assured to the very population driving our climate crisis. While the world's richest 10% caused 52% of emissions between 1990 and 2015, they are also equipped with the resources to fund quick retreats to safety. In 2019, the world's billionaires (2,153 people) had more wealth than 4.6 billion people (over 60% of humanity).

To enable a new development consensus, one that promotes community abundance in alignment with limited planetary resources, globally just green new deals must shake off loan conditions that straightjacket countries - through debt burdens as well as trade and investment structures - from making autonomous decisions about how to increase resilience to climate change impacts.

With fiscal freedom, countries in the Global South could instead eliminate illicit financial flows and seek employment-based and wealth-linked contributions to fund social security, decarbonisation and climate change resilience measures. Funding for fossil fuel, agribusiness and raw earth mineral, metal mining industries, and the military could be redirected. Sovereign wealth funds from debt cancellations could be allocated to the needs and demands of communities on the frontline of climate change impacts. With the freedom to choose a kinder economy, countries could allow for higher budget deficit paths and levels of inflation through a more accommodating macroeconomic framework. These measures are currently restricted under existing trade and investment paradigms but should be sought, while continuing to demand equity fair share based transfers of wealth from the Global North (as discussed in the final chapter). We come back to debt in the final chapter, and consider trade and investment below.

Illustration by Molly Crabapple

4. TRADE & INVESTMENT: BLOCKADING A GLOBAL GREEN NEW DEAL

Across the world, we have seen a rise of political leaders campaigning on a nationalist platform of 'taking back control.' Whilst optically opposed to globalisation, these same leaders are committed to forcing secret trade and investment agreements that prioritise neoliberal privatisation over social protection, enabling a race to the bottom on workers' rights and climate, environmental and food standards. Under these agreements, it becomes systematically difficult for political leaders to genuinely protect civilians from health crises (including Covid-19), economic hardship, and unmitigated climate change. Doing so can elicit legal challenges in secret tribunals through 'investor-state dispute settlements' (ISDS) - a mechanism included in many trade and investment agreements. Several global law firms have predicted that corporations will sue countries for loss of profits due to measures enacted to protect people during the Covid-19 pandemic. Responding to this threat, Sondhya Gupta (UK campaign manager at SumOfUs) told The Guardian:

> *"Clearly, companies shouldn't sue countries over emergency measures to save lives in a global pandemic, and we shouldn't sign trade agreements that let them. We know lower-income countries are struggling most to contain the virus. The threat of rich corporations bullying them out of badly needed public funds to 'compensate' them for profit losses will further hamper efforts to fight the virus and add to the burden on future generations."*[1]

As predicted, Spanish, Canadian, Italian, Dutch, British and US corporations plan to sue governments in the Global South for daring to institute regulations aimed at protecting communities from Covid-19 impacts.[2]

At the same time, the Energy Charter Treaty locks signatories into fossil fuel dependence. In May 2017, UK-based oil and gas company Rockhopper sued Italy after the Italian Parliament banned new oil and gas operations[3] near the country's coast due environmental and earthquake risks. The company demanded compensation for "very significant monetary damages", including lost future profits. The claim was made under the Energy Charter Treaty's investor-to-state dispute settlement (ISDS) mechanism, despite Italy exiting the treaty more than a year before the claim was registered. This is possible as the treaty protects investors for 20 years after a country withdraws from it, thereby instituting investor interests over the popular political will in the long term. Indeed, even if investors lose their claims, states incur significant legal costs in defending health, employment, social protection or climate regulations designed to protect us and our environment. These arbitration mechanisms fail basic standards of judicial independence and fairness, and threaten the responsibility of states to act in the interests of their citizens and the planet. For this reason, public interest groups, trade unions, and academics have called on governments to oppose investor-state arbitration of the type included in the Treaty.[4]

---

1 Doward, Jamie (2020). 'Global Firms Expected to sue UK for Coronavirus Losses.' The Guardian.

2 Olivet, Cecilia & Betina Muller (2020). 'Juggling Crises: Latin America's battle with Covid-19 hampered by investment arbitration cases.' TNI.

3 Thompson, Jennifer and Cat Rutter-Pooley (2017). 'Oil and gas explorer Rockhopper in legal fight with Italy.' Financial Times.

4 Stop ISDS (n.d.). 'Alliance.' Stop ISDS.

Furthermore, intellectual property regimes embedded in trade and investment agreements make it more difficult for people to access affordable medicine, green energy, and prevent farmers from saving seeds. Alongside the race to develop a vaccine for the Covid-19, there is also a rush to patent such developments, which will likely impede universal -- or even widespread - access to what will likely be the world's most in-demand shot. While the development of almost every Covid-19 drug has been made possible by public research and funding, licensing schemes will hand these treatments over to for-profit corporations, who will then control access to what is and should remain a universal public good; allowing them to profit off the pandemic.[5] Rather than learning from the mistakes and missteps of the HIV/AIDs crisis of the 1990s, we are repeating them again.[6]

The well-known violations of labour and environmental standards taking place throughout global supply chains are also actively facilitated by global trade agreements. Goods are made in areas with limited workers' rights and environmental regulations, and almost no enforcement of any local standards - such conditions are implemented in order to offer the promise of cheap land and labour for global corporations.[7] As well as factor labour, international trade requires millions of cheap, informal workers on ports to facilitate the transfer of goods like food, drinks, clothes, jewellery, toys, pharmaceuticals, vehicles, minerals, metals and chemicals. The 'cheapness' of these workers is facilitated by the fact many of them are migrants working in dangerous contexts with limited (or no) state recognised rights, and the fact many of them are racially minoritized women.[8] In other words, they are people who have structurally lower political and social power. At the same time, the pollution produced from shipping these items between ports and where consumers use them are not covered in emissions targets of the Paris Agreement, our international climate change accord.[9] This omission has huge impacts, as the shipping sector emits over 1 billion tonnes of CO_2 a year - more than all but the top

5   Belluz et al. (2020). 'A guide to the vaccines and drugs that could fight Coronavirus.' Vox

6   Ho, Tara Van (2020). 'International Economic Law and Covid-19.' The IEL Collective.

7   Vidal, John (2012). 'Are export processing zones the new sweatshops, or drivers of development?.' The Guardian.

8   Dunaway, Wilma A, ed. (2013). Gendered Commodity Chains: Seeing Women's Work and Households in Global Production. Stanford University Press.

9   Hulac, Benjamin (2015). 'Pollution from planes and ships left out of Paris Agreement.' Scientific American.

five biggest emitting countries.[10] The International Maritime Organisation sees these emissions levels increasing even more over the next decade. While the goods and merchandise move freely, the carbon embedded in their movement is unregulated and the workers that mine, assemble or pack them are often trapped.

In these ways, trade deals systemically entrench global inequality, climate breakdown and worker exploitation. Tackling trade and investment agreements must therefore be an essential step in achieving justice-oriented action on climate change, health inequities and economic injustice. So long as these treaties are intact, genuine advances towards global climate justice are impossible. Indeed, even treaties agreed on the premise that trade should not happen at the expense of the environment or labour conditions, and - on the contrary - promote sustainable development, largely fail to realise that potential.[11] They also fail to acknowledge the historical reasons - rooted colonialism and slavery - why some countries have power to determine the terms of trade and investment, while others have do not. Globally just trade new deals would embed this historical understanding and require a new way of thinking about who has access to what, and the principles underpinning international relations.

More immediately, impact assessments into climate, environmental and labour conditions affected by trade should review the intersecting challenges faced by the paid and unpaid labourers who make global trade possible. Trade agreements can require the reduction of carbon emissions, ensure protection against deforestation, protect the rights of indigenous peoples, require decent work and ensure foreign investors pay towards social protection schemes through proressive forms of taxation. However, the countries that negotiate these trade agreements must not forget their differing responsibilities for funding the work required to transform these commitments from paper to action. Civil society can continue to have a role in monitoring whether trade and investment conditions are being met and require enforcement action through independent, transparent, accessible and binding dispute resolution processes and mechanisms.

---

10 The International Council on Clean Transportation, (October 2013) 'Greenhouse Gas Emissions From Global Shipping, 2013–2015'.

11 Harrison, James and Sophia Paulini (2020). 'The Trade and Sustainable Development Chapter in the EU-Mercosur Association Agreement: Is it fit for purpose?' ClientEarth.

What's wrong with trade and investment agreements?
LAURA BASU

Laura Basu is Europe Editor for Open Democracy, based in Amsterdam, Netherlands.

In times of global pandemic, those wanting to 'take back control' of their democracies would do well to begin with trade and investment agreements. Negotiated in secret, they are tools to transfer power and resources from people to transnational corporations – who are often the only ones in the room. In the new EU-US trade talks replacing TTIP, 90% of European Commission meetings have been found to be with corporate lobbyists.[12]

As well as lowering tariffs, trade deals seek to bring down 'non-tariff barriers' and achieve 'regulatory coherence', promoting a race to the bottom on worker's rights and environmental and food standards. Public services are under threat, as the corporate lobby pushes for liberalisation of all services unless explicitly exempted, including future services.[13] The attack on public services has a particular impact on women, because they are the main users and workers in many of these sectors, and because they remain the main providers of unpaid labour at home or in the community which complements public services. The deals often include 'standstill' or 'ratchet' clauses, meaning that once a sector has been liberalised, it's extremely difficult to go back.

Trade agreements usually include Investor State Dispute Settlements (ISDS), which allow corporations to sue governments for loss of profits, including potential loss of future profits. Governments do not have the reciprocal right to sue corporations. By the end of 2018, states

12 CorporateEurope (2019). 'TTIP reloaded: big business calls the shots on new EU-US trade talks'. CorporateEurope.

13 Fritz, Thomas (2015). 'Public Services Under Attack: TTIP, CETA, and the secretive collusion between business lobbyists and trade negotiators'. CorporateEurope.

worldwide had been ordered or agreed to pay investors USD$88 billion in disclosed ISDS cases.[14]

Research by the Transnational Institute and CEO and reported by openDemocracy has found that law firms are preparing for a 'wave' of such lawsuits in the post-pandemic era, as corporations sue governments for emergency measures brought in to protect populations from the coronavirus. Measures that could face legal challenges include the state acquisition of private hospitals; steps introduced to ensure that drugs, tests and vaccines are affordable; relief on rent, debt and utility payments; and action taken to provide clean water for handwashing.[15]

To date, no other trade and investment agreement has triggered more investor-state lawsuits than the Energy Charter Treaty (ECT) – which has been described as 'the world's most dangerous investment treaty.' Governments attempting to prevent projects that further lock in fossil fuel dependence and accelerate climate change can be held liable for billions in damages under the ECT. Despite its controversy, the ECT is currently expanding, especially in the Global South.[16]

While those pushing these deals claim they are about 'free trade', there is one area in which they promote anything but freedom: intellectual property. Mega-regional trade deals like the Comprehensive and Progressive Agreement for Trans-Pacific Partnership include intellectual property protections that go way beyond WTO rules, and these provisions are replicated in multiplying bilateral and regional treaties. They make it more difficult for people to access to affordable medicine, prevent farmers from saving seeds, and open the way to genetically modified organisms.[17]

Trade deals entrench global imbalances and reinforce the international division of labour, standing in the way of a globally just Green New Deal. In RCEP – a mega-regional trade deal currently being negotiated among 16 countries across Asia-Pacific – it is the corporations of big players like China, Japan, New Zealand and Australia

---

14 Olivet et al. (2020). 'Pandemic Profiteers: How foreign investors could make billions from crisis measures.' TNI.

15 Basu et al. (2020). 'Exclusive: Countries to face a 'wave' of corporate lawsuits challenging emergency Covid-19 measures.' OpenDemocracy.

16 ECT's Dirty Secrets (2019). 'What is the Energy Charter Treaty?. ECT's Dirty Secrets.

17 GRAIN (2017). 'How RCEP affects food and farmers.' GRAIN.

who will benefit from the further opening up of key markets to large corporations, driving out the small family farms that produce 80% of the region's food. RCEP will also enable land grabbing, as vast tracts of land are bought up by foreign multinationals where currently in many countries investors can only lease land.[18]

Unfortunately, deals negotiated behind closed doors in the presence of corporate lobbyists to shift wealth and power to giant corporations do not tend to bode well for people or planet. Tackling trade and investment agreements[19] will be an essential first step in achieving transnational and justice-oriented action on climate change in a post-Covid world. ●

In the piece below Cecila Oliveta and Lucía Bárcena from the Transnational Institute outline the specific obstacles to achieving a Green New Deal under the Energy Charter Treaty.

How investment treaties could blockade a Green New Deal
CECILIA OLIVET & LUCÍA BÁRCENA

Cecilia Olivet is Coordinator for Trade And Investment Programme at Transnational Institute, based in Belgium; and Lucía Bárcena is Project Officer for Trade And Investment Programme at Transnational Institute, based in Spain.

Leaving fossil fuels in the ground is a key requirement to limit global warming to 2°C, according to climate scientists. The majority of European parliamentarians recently joined the call for fossil fuel phase

18 Ibid.

19 Poojaffd (2020). 'Stop all trade and investment treaty negotiations during the Covid-19 outbreak.' Civil Society Financing for Development (FFD) Group.

out. Yet, most governments are failing to implement an energy transition. Instead of banning new permits for exploration or extraction of fossil fuels, limiting or rescinding existing licenses, cutting subsidies to coal, gas or oil; or taxing its production, a recent UN report warns that "governments are planning to produce about 50% more fossil fuels in 2030 than would be consistent with limiting warming to 2°C and 120% more than would be consistent with limiting warming to 1.5°C".[20]

Many factors deter government action to tackle the fossil fuel industry. But there is one obstacle that is rarely talked about. International investment treaties, in particular the Energy Charter Treaty (ECT),[21] are powerful weapons for fossil fuel corporations. They enable them to attack any climate measure that could reduce their profits, even those enacted to deal with the social and ecological crisis.

How are fossil fuels investors using investment agreements to prevent an energy transition?

Using investment agreements, fossil fuel companies can deter governments from advancing climate legislation, or make steps towards energy transition extremely expensive.

Big oil, gas and coal companies can bypass national legal systems. Instead, they can use a web of over 2600 international investment treaties[22] to sue States for billions of dollars in "damages" at international arbitration tribunals if governments move to shut down or restrict the profits of fossil fuel projects. Environmental lawyer Amandine Van Den Berghe, summed up the problem: "fossil fuel companies may seek to use ISDS to shift their losses from stranded assets onto states and seek unmerited compensation for poor business decisions".

The Energy Charter Treaty is the world's most dangerous investment agreement, due to its wide geographical reach and its extremely broad and generous investor privileges. Created in the 1990s to protect

---

20 SEI, IISD, ODI, Climate Analytics, CICERO, and UNEP (2019). 'The Production Gap: the discrepancy between countries' planned fossil fuel production and global production consistent with limiting warming to 1.5°C or 2°C'. The Production Gap.

21 ECT's Dirty Secrets (2019). 'What is the Energy Charter Treaty?. ECT's Dirty Secrets.

22 ECT's Dirty Secrets (2019). 'What is the Energy Charter Treaty?. ECT's Dirty Secrets.

foreign investors in the energy sector, it has since been used in 131 cases by investors to sue States.[23]

Several of these lawsuits were initiated by fossil fuel companies attempting to undermine governments' efforts to fight climate change. In 2017, Italy was sued by the British oil and gas company Rockhopper after cancelling its concession to drill oil in the Adriatic Sea. This followed a decade of struggle by Italian coastal communities who denounced the danger of coastal drilling, which had already caused earthquakes and threatened new ecological disasters. The oil company is using the Energy Charter Treaty to demand 300 million euros in compensation - seven times the amount the company initially invested.

This case, like the 1,000 other investment treaty lawsuits[24] *known about worldwide, will be decided by three private lawyers acting as arbitrators. These arbitrators tend to defend private investor rights above public interest,*[25] *revealing an inherent pro-corporate bias. Their decisions are binding and immediately enforceable. Arbitrators' rulings usually ignore the public interest concerns motivating the government's intervention, or the fact that the companies may well have been fully aware of the risks*[26] *when they invested.*

Fossil fuel companies are also using the threat of billion-dollar lawsuits to dissuade governments from taking effective climate action. Canadian oil and gas company Vermillion, which extracts almost 75% of all French oil, used the threat of an ECT lawsuit to dissuade the French government from legislating to phase out fossil fuel extraction. The law was shelved and replaced by a watered-down version which continues to allow it. More recently, German coal giant Uniper threatened to sue the Netherlands for up to €1 billion over a new law banning the use of coal for electricity production by 2030.[27] *The threat was made when the law was being discussed by the Dutch Parliament. Even though the threat didn't stop the proposal becoming law, the*

23 International Energy Charter (2020). 'List of cases'. International Energy Charter.

24 UNCTAD (n.d.). 'Investment Dispute Settlement Navigator'. UN.

25 Olivet, Cecilia and Pia Eberhardt (2012). 'Profiting from injustice: How law firms, arbitrators and financiers are fuelling an investment arbitration boom'. TNI.

26 Olivet, Cecilia and Pia Eberhardt (2014). 'Profiting from crisis: How corporations and lawyers are scavenging profits from Europe's crisis countries'. TNI.

27 Darby, Megan (2020). 'Coal generator uses investment treaty to fight Netherlands coal phaseout'. Climate Home News.

intent to chill legislation was clear - and the company might still follow through.

In an era of climate crisis, it is almost inconceivable that governments are still subsidising dirty energy. Yet, if they start to cut subsidies to coal, gas or oil, it is likely that States will see an avalanche of investment lawsuits. Spain has been sued 47 times over cuts to renewable energy subsidies. Cuts to subsidies of any type of energy could unleash the same result.

The costs of investment lawsuits run into billions of US dollars and could bring the budgets of most countries, particularly in the Global South, to breaking point. By the end of 2018, States worldwide had been ordered or agreed to pay investors a staggering USD$88 billion due to ISDS cases. This money could otherwise have been spent on climate adaptation and funding energy transition. To put this in perspective, the Adaptation Fund, one of the main multilateral climate funds, has committed to USD$ 720 million for different projects since 2010. This is less than 1% of what governments had to pay foreign investors as a result of ISDS cases.

Are energy transition friendly investment agreements possible?

The short answer is no. There are many other legal instruments that could support an energy transition - we don't need investment treaties, even reformed and improved ones.[28]

International investment agreements (IIAs) were largely signed because governments believed they would help States attract foreign direct investment (FDI). Yet, years of research and ample experience has shown that IIAs are not a determining factor in the attraction of FDI, including clean energy investment as is claimed nowadays. So, all that remains for States is the risk of being sued.

IIAs only protect foreign investors. They don't include any obligations, and only investors can initiate lawsuits. In particular, they protect large transnational corporations. The fossil fuel industry has initiated at least 150 ISDS lawsuits, making it one of the most prolific users of the

28 Fossil Fuel Treaty (n.d.). 'The Fossil Fuel Non-Proliferation Treaty.' Fossil Fuel Treaty.

*system. Yet, transnational corporations, in particular fossil fuel compa-
nies, surely don't need, and shouldn't enjoy, extra protection.*

*Governments in India, Morocco and even the Southern African
Development Community (SADC) have promoted "alternative" models
of investment agreements. But while these new treaties might reduce
the risk of being sued, they do not alter the nature of investment
agreements and could still hinder governments' efforts to address
climate breakdown.*

*Investment protection treaties are not just shields that protect the
fossil fuel industry, they are powerful swords that empower them to
attack governments trying to act on climate change. The international
investment regime is not compatible with an energy transition or a
green new deal. Keeping it in place will only extend the fossil fuel era.*

*The solution to predatory investment treaties is not better agree-
ments that "reduce" the risk for States. The solution is for governments
to follow the example of South Africa, Indonesia, Ecuador, Italy or even
all EU member States. They must urgently terminate all international
investment treaties in force, in particular the Energy Charter Treaty,
and stop negotiating new ones. Only then will governments be able to
phase out fossil fuels and truly advance a green new deal without the
risk of having to spend millions of euros compensating corporations.* ●

While corporations can bring expensive arbitration claims and have the
decision of secretive panels be binding on the citizens and government of
nations without accountability, the Paris Agreement and human rights treaties
lack the same agency.

In the piece below, Donatella Alessandrini describes the historic and continuing injustices upon which trade negotiations take place. Slavery, colonialism and unpaid labour are significant contexts. The British fought three wars
to gain access to Burmese forests. Ten million people - half the population of
Congo at the time - died as Belgium took hold of rubber and ivory subjecting
local people to a ruthless regime. Twelve million people - predominantly from
West Africa - were shackled into boats headed for the Americas where they
were forced into silver and gold mines, and various crop plantations. Forests
were cleared to make way for livestock and sugar cane plantations. Goods
made for export. In the last decades of the 19th century, tens of millions of

Indian died of famine, while British colonial policy forced the country to export record levels of food. These numbers cannot bring to life the devastation experienced by people, families and places, and the loss of diverse cosmologies promoting interdependence, stewardship, and non-binary concepts of work, gender, sexuality and more. Colonialism reconfigured the world economy. India's share of the global economy shrank from 27 to 3%. It is estimated that the UK benefited by approximately USD$45 trillion from its colonial rule of the Indian subcontinent alone. China's share shrank from 35 to 7%. At the same time, Europe's share exploded from 20 to 60%. In addition to the natural and human impacts, this funded industrialisation and the early industrialisers were responsible for more than three times as many GHG emissions between 1850 and 2002 than so called developing countries. Experience of colonial practices continue to be strong indicators of poverty today, and poverty increases susceptibility to climate change impacts.

Similarly, for too long women's subsistence labour - collecting firewood, growing food for family consumption, collecting water (increasingly difficult in regions subject to water insecurity), care work and more - has been unpaid. This labour has not only been undervalued and undermined, but is required to create a new generation of labourers. Women's participation in paid labour often justifies sweatshop labour. However, this participation often takes place in precarious contexts.

Not only do existing trade and investment schemes - built on free trade ideologies - entrench labour precarity and highlight gender injustice, they also kick away the ladder to development for developing countries.[29] Research from Global Justice Now indicated that African countries receive $161.6 billion in resources such as loans, remittances and aid each year, but lose $203 billion through factors including tax avoidance, debt payments and resource extraction, creating an annual net financial deficit of over $40 billion.

---

29 Chang, Ha-Joon (20020). 'Kicking away the ladder: An unofficial history of capitalism, especially in Britain and the United States.' Challenge Journal 45(5).

Illustration by Tomekah George

Trade treaties, comparative advantage and social inequalities
DONATELLA ALESSANDRINI

Donatella Alessandrini is a Professor Of Law at University Of Kent in Canterbury, UK.

International trade and investment treaties are built on the problematic assumption that countries trade with one another because they have different competitive advantages which can be exchanged to everyone's mutual benefit. The problem with this assumption is that it fails to articulate how various advantages came about. The ways in which states and corporations come to gain specific competitive advantages are through processes permeated by social inequalities, including gender and racial inequalities. Underpinning gender inequalities in the labour market, as feminist economists have argued, is the pursuit of competitive advantage by avoiding paying towards the full costs of the reproduction of the labour force and of our planet. For example firms may establish themselves in jurisdictions where they pay less tax, which has a negative impact on the revenue available to provide local public education, health services and, crucially, environmental standards. Multinational corporations also create complex supply webs to push any costs of contributing in these ways to local contractors who then squeeze the labour force and exploit or neglect the environment in order to extract profits on small operating revenues, while big brands take the bulk of the trade benefit.

The way in which workers and the environment are treated and regulated is constitutive of what we call competitive advantage, rather than being its consequence or 'externality'. The pressure on firms and states to abide by the 'commercial provisions' of trade and investment treaties (to say nothing of the private contracts signed between firms) means that, unless the contribution workers and the environment make to production and trade is properly acknowledged, treated and remunerated, its invisibilization and/or devaluation will continue to provide a source of competitiveness in the global economy.

How, then, can this contribution be acknowledged in international trade regulation so that 'employment', 'environmental protection' and 'gender equality' concerns - to use the terminology of these treaties - can transform the substance of 'commercial provisions'? If we start from the premise that the composition and conditions of re/productive labour vary from country to country, depending on gender, class, race, ethnicity, migration flows and so on, and that resources are unequally distributed between and within the Global South and Global North, then uniform and universal environmental and labour regulation through multilateral trade rules is undesirable, particularly when linked to trade sanctions. What is possible and necessary, however, is to hold the 'commercial provisions' of current trade treaties to account, and we can start by scrutinizing their effects on environmental, working and living conditions. A further step would involve re-thinking trade treaties and commercial relations more broadly, putting decent environmental, working and living conditions, rather than global competition and capital accumulation, at the centre of trade policies. ●

Illustration by Molly Crabapple

5. THIS LAND IS OUR LAND: CONSERVATION, FOOD AND ENERGY

The way we are using land is accelerating the climate crisis. The ability of communities around the world to live autonomously and harmoniously on the land to which they are tied is routinely and violently intercepted by multinational corporations in the name of conservation and food and energy provision. Yet, the same communities in the Global South whose land is grabbed under international trade and investment agreements for these purposes, are the same communities systematically denied from the harvests exported from places that have been taken. The global food system is driving environmental injustice through extreme water use, the pollution of ecosystems by pesticides and agricultural run-off and producing roughly a quarter of the world's greenhouse gas emissions.[1]

In the last two decades, it is estimated that 26.7 million hectares of land has been acquired by foreign investors for use in the agriculture business.[2]

---

1   Ritchie, Hannah (2019). 'Food production is responsible for one-quarter of the world's greenhouse gas emissions.' Our World in Data, Oxford Martin School.

2   Nolte et al. (2016). 'International Land Deals for Agriculture. Fresh Insights from the Land Matrix: Analytic Report II.' Land Matrix.

Yet, the global, multinational corporation driven agricultural industry - which we refer to as agribusiness - implicated in these acquisitions, has only become more inefficient, unequal, polluting and reliant on displacement. Much of this is rooted in the unevenness of land ownership, where industrial commodity crop farms have taken land away from those who use it for direct, local food production, and who often have spiritual, cultural and ancestral connections to the land.

Many of these commodity crop farms use vast swathes of land for the production of just one crop, like palm oil or sugar, which places a huge toll on the health of the soil and its ability to support diverse plant growth later. According to GRAIN, small farms make up 90% of all farms - and yet these small farmers have just 25% of the world's farmland to work on.[3] Indeed, small farmers - mainly women - feed most of the world on less than a quarter of all agricultural land. The large agribusinesses that own the majority of the land and control trade in grain, biotech and industrial food production force out local food producers and impoverished people, and drive environmental degradation with the highly polluting activities and intensive water use at the core of their practice. Workers in the industry also continue to rank among the world's most insecure workforces. The International Labour Organization (ILO) estimates that at least 170,000 workers in the agricultural sector are killed each year - whether through lack of protections, higher risk of poverty or exposure to toxic pesticides.[4] Meanwhile, indigenous peoples are custodians of 80% of the world's remaining biodiversity, but are facing severe food insecurity, extreme poverty and other human rights deprivations.

Agribusiness fundamentally fails to adequately fulfil the food needs of the worlds' population - one in three people face some form of malnourishment, and one in nine face hunger issues.[5] The 'supermarketisation' of food systems leads to an increase in reliance on processed, rather than fresh, food - contributing to this rise in malnutrition and obesity. Children remain the most vulnerable to malnutrition - according to the World Health Organization, malnutrition is the underlying contributing factor in approximately 45% of deaths of children under five.[6] Today's food systems are dominated by trade

---

3 GRAIN (2014). 'Hungry for land: small farmers feed the world with less than a quarter of all farmland.' GRAIN.

4 ILO (2015). 'Agriculture: A Hazardous Work.' ILO.

5 WFP (2019). '2019 - Hunger Map.' UN: World Food Programme.

6 FCRN Food Source (2018). 'What is malnutrition?.' Environmental Change Institute, University of Oxford.

agreements and economic policies that prioritize profits over the right to food. Power is concentrated in the hands of a few corporate actors that benefit from free trade rules and export-oriented agricultural policies. Such regimes privilege large-scale agribusinesses to the detriment of others, creating instability in the global food system. Yet, the food produced in this way represents a small part of global production - the UN estimates that 70-80% of the food consumed in most of the Global South is produced by smallholder farms.[7] The 20-30% of food produced by large agri-businesses is having huge, destructive impacts across the system.

Big commodity traders like Bunge Ltd, Cargill, Luis Dreyfus and Archer Daniels Midland, are the agricultural equivalents of fossil fuel companies like Shell and BP. They reap the rewards of a broken system and are subsidised by state handouts, while leaving the basic needs of millions unfulfilled and destroying the natural world. Trade agreements encourage the planting of cash crops and the industrial meat industry, thereby incentivising deforestation, the redirection of water away from local communities and the pollution of ecosystems. Indeed, the destruction of forests in order to grow animal feed is one of the biggest threats to biodiversity, which is vital to sustainable agriculture, resilient and sustainable food production, and carbon sequestration.

This process also results in the marginalization of women from agricultural decision-making, whose subsistence-based knowledge and practices are derided and made impossible. Women face a lack of voice in shaping work agendas, and increasingly depend on men for cash and access to the market to purchase the food they previously grew. This contributes to a growing dissonance between women's roles as agriculturalists and the social recognition accorded to them, and has particularly troubling implications for household food security, since the main responsibility for this lies in women's hands.[8] It also prioritises business-led ways of knowing and doing over more sustainable methods, like traditional rotational systems, permanent pasture and conservation grazing. These sustainable forms of farming that can restore soils and biodiversity, and sequester carbon, are derided, while the demand for crops requiring high inputs of fertiliser, fungicides, pesticides and herbicides are forcibly increased. The growing feminization and casualization of

---

7 UNFAO (2014). 'The state of food and agriculture 2014: In brief.' Food and Agriculture Organization of the United Nations.

8 Harcourt, Wendy and Ingrid L. Nelson, eds (2015). Practising Feminist Political Ecologies: Moving Beyond the 'Green Economy.' Zed Books.

the waged agricultural workforce over the past few years enables flexibility for larger growers, while increasing precarity for workers.

The ecological cost of agribusiness is also clear. As a model, agribusiness dangerously increases emissions while destroying wild habitats - and by driving climate breakdown, the agricultural industry is, somewhat ironically, making access to food increasingly precarious. As a recent example, Cyclone Idai (which struck Mozambique, Malawi and Zimbabwe in March 2019) alone destroyed nearly two million acres of crops including corn, cassava, beans, rice and groundnuts such as peanuts. Displacement caused by increased frequency and intensity of extreme weather is being particularly felt by those who rely on the fishing and agriculture sector for income and subsistence.

Industrial agricultural practices also threaten food stability by reducing our resilience to intensifying ecological impacts - such as desertification - in the future. A 2015 report from the UN Food and Agriculture Organization found that, globally, 25 to 40 billion tonnes of topsoil are lost annually to erosion, thanks mainly to ploughing and intensive cropping.[9] The IPCC's August 2019 Special Report on Climate Change and Land found that to become fit for purpose in an era of climate change, agriculture must move away from intensive and industrialised approaches, and towards food systems based on agroecology and less and better meat.[10]

Countries on the frontline of the most extreme impacts have done very little to cause the crisis and instead been required (through trade and investment agreements) to open their markets to foreign investment in a carbon intensive, displacing and polluting way of growing food. A vicious and ironic cycle, where global agribusiness is behind some of the biggest threats to food sustainability and accessibility, is therefore coded in the DNA of our global food system. The Special Rapporteur on Extreme Poverty and Human Rights warns that this is leading towards a "climate apartheid scenario in which the wealthy pay to escape overheating, hunger and conflict, while the rest of the world is left to suffer". [11]

In response to this crisis, the international peasant movement La Vía Campesina developed the concept of 'food sovereignty' in the 1990s.[12] Introduced

---

9   UNFAO (2015). 'Soils are endangered, but the degradation can be rolled back'. Food and Agriculture Organization of the United Nations.

10 IPCC (2019). 'Climate Change and Land'. IPCC.

11 UN (2019). 'World faces 'climate apartheid' risk, 120 more million in poverty: UN expert'. UN News.

12 Viacampesina.org

Illustration by Tomekah George

at the World Food Summit in 1996, food sovereignty was framed as an explicit critique of the neoliberal global food system[13], representing a radical break with the dominant agrarian system. The 2007 Nyeleni Declaration defines food sovereignty as "the right of peoples to healthy and culturally appropriate food produced through ecologically sound and sustainable methods, and their right to define their own food and agriculture systems."[14] Food sovereignty prioritizes factors such as local production, direct commercialization, the use of agroecological methods, opposition to genetically modified crops and agro-chemicals, and rights to land, water, seeds and biodiversity.

A globally just Green New Deal must think of land and food as part of the global commons, and therefore to be regulated and shared fairly.[15] It must also recognise the intimate relationship between land sovereignty and food justice. This means supporting indigenous land rights, halting land grabs for mining, agro-industrial plantations and biofuels and banning land speculation by big financial institutions. Supporting regional, short and regenerative agro-ecological models, as well as traditional knowledge that minimises the use of toxic

13 La Vía Campesina (2003). 'Food sovereignty.' La Via Campesina.

14 Nyéléni Forum 2007 (2007). 'Declaration of Nyéléni.' Nyéléni.

15 Vivero-Pol et al. (2018). Routledge Handbook of Food as a Commons. Taylor & Francis.

inputs, reduces food waste and re-allocates industrial agriculture subsidies to small farmers, would not only cool the planet, but feed the world at least three times over.[16] It is entirely possible to live in a world where everyone has access to publicly paid for food. Agricultural policies across 53 countries currently provide an average of USD$528 billion per-year of direct support to - predominantly intensive - agricultural businesses.[17] These resources must be redirected to climate change resilient and equitable practices. In addition, while it is no substitute for land and resource redistribution, any technological innovations, such as plant-based meat alternatives, must be accessible to all those who need and want it.

Taking the agricultural industries into public ownership, re-thinking what we produce and how much we really need, democratising land access and control of food decision making to prioritise sustenance over market power is crucial, especially for revaluing the labour rights of a women-dominated workforce and enabling food justice. Embracing this kind of 'food citizenship' may take many forms,[18] including support for greater urban-rural engagement, collective procurement and participation in food policy councils. Such community-based movements are taking control of local and regional food systems with the goal of promoting bottom-up change. Indeed, the food and energy needs of the world's population do not contradict principles of land sovereignty, which holds that "land belongs to those who work it, care for it and live on it".[19] On the contrary; a Global Green New Deal that enshrines land sovereignty is necessary to achieve a just new deal.

16 Erdman, Jeremy (2018). 'We produce enough food to feed 10 billion people. So why does hunger still exist?'. Jeremy Edman.

17 OECD (2019). 'Agricultural Policy Monitoring and Evaluation 2019'. OECD iLibrary.

18 Lozano-Cabedo, Carmen and Cristobal Gomez-Benito (2017). 'A theoretical model of food citizenship for the analysis of social praxis'. Journal of Agricultural and Environmental Ethics 30(1), p1-22.

19 Borras Jr, Santurnino and Jennifer C. Franco (2012). 'A 'Land Sovereignty' Alternative: Towards a Peoples' Counter-Enclosure'. TNI.

Nothing about us without us: centring workers in the just agriculture transition
TERESA ANDERSON

Teresa Anderson is a Climate Policy Coordinator for Action Aid International, based in Johannesburg, South Africa.

Agriculture is a major source of the world's greenhouse gases, and is highly vulnerable to its impacts. At the same time, agriculture is the source of food security for almost everyone on earth, the basis for the livelihoods for more than 1 billion people, and the foundation of many economies. Dramatically cutting greenhouse gases (GHGs) in the agriculture sector could thus bring major disruptions to peoples' lives and food security if done without prudence. The transition in agriculture must therefore be undertaken with care, ensuring that considerations of justice and rights are central to the approach. The following "Principles for a Just Transition in Agriculture"[20]have been developed by ActionAid, to help guide this necessary shift:

1. Transform the food system to work for people, nature and the climate.

The IPCC Special Report on Climate Change and Land (August 2018) confirms that to become fit for purpose in an era of climate change, agriculture must move away from intensive and industrialised approaches, and towards food systems based on agroecology and less and better meat. The term "agroecology" describes a set of agricultural practices that work with nature and largely avoid GHG emissions by improving soil health, crop diversity, resilience to pests and disease, and avoiding the use of chemical fertilisers and pesticides. With 70% of the world's cropland currently used for producing livestock feed, shifting away from industrial and large-scale livestock production

20 Borras Jr, Santurnino and Jennifer C. Franco (2012). 'A 'Land Sovereignty' Alternative: Towards a Peoples' Counter-Enclosure.' TNI.

and consumption has also been identified as a necessary measure to reduce the industry's outsize contribution to methane, deforestation and land use.

2. Address – don't exacerbate – inequalities.

One of the major challenges to changing agricultural practices is that farmers using industrial agriculture techniques can feel demonised and defensive that they are being blamed for the climate crisis. They may be wary that top-down and simplistic climate policies will leave large sections of rural communities stranded, with few options for secure livelihoods. There is already deep injustice across the food system, with farmers and workers often squeezed and exploited by a system that concentrates wealth, land and power in fewer and fewer hands. Women farmers face particular barriers and burdens. Meanwhile, two billion people are still food insecure. A just transition in agriculture must therefore be done in a way that addresses – and does not exacerbate – injustices in the food system.

3. Ensure inclusiveness and participation.

The term "just transition," originally coined by unions, defines WHAT the new system will look like, and HOW that transformation is carried out. A just transition must be genuinely inclusive and participatory, engaging with key actors, particularly those that are marginalised and ignored such as women farmers. Farmers, workers and communities must be given a seat at the table and opportunities to shape their own future.

4. Develop a comprehensive framework.

Governments should develop comprehensive policy frameworks that provide positive opportunities for better food systems that work for farmers and the climate. Regional and national level impact assessments and planning processes, gender-responsive and inclusive policies, social protection, training and reskilling, support for new routes to market, as well as joined-up thinking that links different sectors and global connections will be key. These elements can form the basis of increasingly ambitious national climate policies including Nationally Determined Contributions (NDCs) and National Adaptation Plans (NAPs).

Through a just transition in agriculture, many communities that might otherwise resist climate action can become powerful advocates for change. ●

In 2019, the burning of the Amazon and the darkening of skies from Sao Paulo, Brazil, to Santa Cruz, Bolivia, captured the world's conscience. Much of the blame rightly fell on Brazilian President Jair Bolsonaro for encouraging the burning of forests and the seizure of Indigenous Peoples' lands. Less reported was the fact that this is incentivised by large-scale international meat and soy animal feed companies like JBS and Cargill, and the global brands like Stop & Shop, Costco, McDonald's, Walmart/Asda, and Sysco that buy from them and sell to the public. These companies are creating the international demand that finances the fires and deforestation.

From the Greater Mekong, to the Amazon and Madagascar, alarming reports have emerged of increased poaching, illegal logging and forest fires, while many countries are engaging in hasty environmental rollbacks and cuts in funding for ecological protection. Deforestation and forest degradation in the tropics account for a significant share of global carbon emissions. This all comes at a time when we need these spiritual sites, homes to vast species and carbon absorbers the most. Existing schemes, such as the REDD scheme and REDD+ are insufficient to prevent this, worse, conservation schemes can actively harm those that have done the most to protect our remaining social and planetary biodiversity.

The REDD+ scheme (Reducing Emissions through Deforestation and Degradation) is in the Bali Action Plan, and UNFCCC parties have agreed to consider REDD+ forest carbon schemes as a potential way to mitigate and offset carbon emissions and enhance forest carbon stocks in developing countries. Supported by the World Bank, FAO, UN Environment Programme (UNEP) and UN Development Programme (UNDP), REDD+ projects involve host governments and forest-dependent communities (largely in developing countries) being paid small sums via complex market-based mechanisms to reduce carbon emissions from deforestation and forest degradation, and for conserving, managing and enhancing carbon stocks. While some projects included reduction aims, most focused on conservation.

The social impacts of REDD and REDD+ projects on people living in and around forest areas, however, have often not been taken into consideration. In a number of African countries, these projects even enabled states to grab land from indigenous and forest communities without seeking full prior and informed consent[21] - despite this being required as part of the UN Declaration on the Rights of Indigenous Peoples. The UN Committee on the Elimination of Racial Discrimination, issued concerns around the implementation of REDD activities in Indonesia, given the impact on indigenous peoples' right to possess, develop, control and use their communal land. Action Aid have reported forced evictions and human rights violations, lost livelihoods, divided communities, destruction of culturally significant sites and increased poverty - all of which disproportionately impact women, who undertake the majority of household food production.[22]

Indigenous and forest peoples have understood and managed their environment best, evidenced by the fact that 80% of Earth's biodiversity is in tribal territories. When indigenous peoples have secure rights over their land, they achieve at least equal if not better conservation results at a fraction of the cost of conventional conservation programs. But in Africa and Asia, governments and NGOs are stealing vast areas of land from tribal people and local communities under the false claim that this is necessary for conservation. The grabbed land is called a "Protected Area" or "National Park" and the original inhabitants dispossessed, sometimes with shocking violence. Tourists are welcomed and trophy hunting, logging, and mining have been known to take place within these taken territories. Ecoguards and park rangers have been known to target local people's assets and torture with impunity. In February 2020, Survival International research implicated the WWF in funding so-called "ecoguards" who have been accused of torturing the forest communities that have long relied on, and protected, the Messok Dja area of the Republic of Congo.[23] Similar stories of forest peoples being displaced and then tortured

21 REDD-Monitor (2015). Carbon Conflicts and Forest Landscapes in Africa. REDD-Monitor.

22 Oram, Julian (2014). 'The Great Land Heist: How the world is paving the way for corporate land grabs'. ActionAid.

23 Lang, Chris (2020). 'UNDP investigation confirms that WWF-funded ecoguards beat up indigenous people in the Republic of Congo'. Redd-Monitor.

for entering their previous territories, even for collecting snails, have been made in Nepal.[24]

Multinational institutions such as the World Bank have promoted participatory learning and action or gender and development methods to elicit input in projects from local communities. However, these approaches tend towards maintaining predominant economic growth models that elicit particular, strategically beneficial voices from communities to do so. They fail to call into question the view that the environment can be a commodity for trade or a state's property, therefore avoid proposing solutions that could lead to substantial political and economic transformation and justice. Depending on how it is done, participation can either come from a desire to protect autonomy, or it can be designed to legitimise the prioritisation of economic growth over people and planet. At its worst, the co-option of 'participation' can continue the prevailing mantra of growth-centred economics - which itself has caused the crisis - thereby failing to empower local people and continuing Eurocentric conceptions of development.[25]

A Global Green New Deal must learn from the mistakes of programmes like REDD and REDD+, and ensure meaningful democratic participation of indigenous and forest-dependent communities when engaging with questions of land conservation, including decision-making say over whether land is traded, parcelled, and financialized at all. Participation of women, indigenous communities and forest peoples within schemes that subordinate to market norms does not allow for decision-making which rejects colonized conceptions of ownership in favour of a deep recognition of our interdependence and reliance on land, and for the protection of our commons.

Market-based solutions to our crisis will fail. Commodification, trading and financialization of nature and ecosystemic regeneration are part and parcel of the ongoing drive of capitalism towards an 'accumulation by dispossession.' Everything from the regeneration of nature, global natural commons, public goods and state-run enterprises and facilities, social reproduction, care and social relations become marketised. The climate change negotiations nurture the concept of green commodification through carbon trading, joint implementation and the Clean Development Mechanisms (like REDD, REDD+ among

---

24 Warren, Tom and Katie J.M. Baker (2019). 'WWF Funds Guards who have Tortured and Killed People.' Buzzfeed.

25 Richards, P (1995). 'Participatory Rural Appraisal: A quick and dirty critique.' PLA Notes

others). They open a huge segment for the financial market. At the Rio+20 conference, banks, investment funds and insurance companies signed up to a 'Natural Capital Declaration' for the purpose of integrating natural capital into their financial valuations. Techno-science like genetic manipulation and gene editing , and geo-engineering new technologies for resource extractivism from fracking to deep-sea mining and for substitution of natural processes as in synthetic biology, nanotechnology and reproductive technologies intensify the ongoing commodification. They facilitate the adjustment of nature, human nature and the social to the neoliberal market rationale for monetary price, efficiency and profitability.[26] A Global Green New Deal contains within it the hopes of reversing the intensification of neoliberal market approaches towards nature, gender, indigeneity, poverty, labour and social justice concerns.

REDD+ and the failures in land diversity ambitions
ALEX WIJERATNA

Alex Wijeratna is a Campaign Director for Mighty Earth, based in UK.

> Based on my reading of REDD+ carbon offset schemes over the last 10 years or so, I am alarmed by the impacts of REDD+ on the rights of Indigenous and local communities on the ground, and I'm increasingly dubious that i) they work in carbon terms, and ii) can deliver zero deforestation and the necessary forest finance at the speed and scale that we need for a 1.5C world.
>
> Global peasants movements, community-based (CBOs) and civil society organisations (CSOs) see REDD+ as another form of commodification and privatization of the commons and point to first-hand and extensive documented evidence that pilot REDD+ forest carbon schemes are simply not working – for local forest-dependent com-

26 Harcourt, Wendy and Ingrid L. Nelson, eds (2015). Practising Feminist Political Ecologies: Moving Beyond the 'Green Economy.' Zed Books.

munities or in climate change terms. A significant number of studies show that REDD+ schemes promote land grabs and human rights abuses, cause conflict over Indigenous and customary land rights, create disputes over carbon rights, carbon credits, carbon leakage and community compensation payments. They are riddled by weak governance, weak participation and 'elite capture', and increase discrimination against rural women, tribal and Indigenous peoples. Under REDD+ schemes, the rights of affected Indigenous and local communities to Free, Prior and Informed Consent (FPIC) are rarely carried out, and a wealth of evidence shows that Indigenous peoples, shifting cultivators and rural women lose out in particular. ●

Yet, rather than learning from past mistakes, the Paris Agreement has systematised reliance on market driven mechanisms through the Sustainable Development Mechanism of the Paris Agreement. In the piece below, Nathan Thanki outlines how it does this, and what the justice centred demands and alternatives are.

Justice alternatives to the Sustainable Development Mechanism of the Paris Agreement
NATHAN THANKI

Nathan Thanki is a Co-Coordinator for Global Campaign To Demand Climate Justice, based in London, UK.

The Paris Agreement differs from the Kyoto Protocol in several regards. It both weakens the differentiation between developed and developing countries and abandons the collective setting of targets and timetables for emissions reductions in favour of the far more flexible approach of "nationally determined contributions" (NDCs). The result, famously, is that everyone is on board but the ship is sinking: even if

*the NDCs are implemented, temperatures are on track to rise by 3-4°C
this century.*

*One area in which the Paris Agreement does mimic the Kyoto
Protocol is in the use of market-based approaches to climate change
mitigation. The Kyoto Protocol's so-called "Clean Development Mechanism" was tainted by questions over its efficacy and many instances of
human rights abuses and land grabs particularly impacting indigenous
peoples and forest communities. Emissions trading schemes demon-
strably failed to reduce emissions. Yet the Paris Agreement (specifically,
Article 6) persists in relying on these policy approaches that are proven
failures.*

*Article 6 is couched in the language of "voluntary cooperation"
but this is code for the same kind of logic that underpinned the indul-
gences of the Middle Ages' Catholic Church; those who can afford to
pay are absolved of their sins. The poor pick up the burden. The basic
premise of this kind of 'cooperation' is that countries are able to use
"internationally transferred mitigation outcomes" to count towards
their NDC. So, if a developed country wanted to, it could increase its
own carbon-intensive activities and simply purchase the right to offset
this pollution through mitigation carried out in another country. One
of the technologies touted to deliver these offsets is Bioenergy with
Carbon Capture and Storage (BECCS). In theory, BECCS would involve
planting trees to absorb atmospheric carbon, cutting those trees down
and burning the biomass to use the energy, then somehow capturing
and storing the carbon in the ground. There are a plethora of problems.
Bioenergy is not actually carbon neutral. The technology doesn't exist
at scale yet, and to scale it up would require vast amounts of land.
Whose land? You can easily guess.*

*Rather than persist in a near-fanatical commitment to market-based
false solutions, climate justice demands real solutions which are
people-centred and equitable which are people-centred and equitable,
and which appreciate the inherent value of nature rather than reduce
it to a commodity. Some solutions include, but are not limited to:
drastically limiting corporations and wealthy elites excessive consumption, particularly of energy; removing barriers to affordable and
accessible environmentally sound technologies such as intellectual
property rights; ending producer subsidies promoting fossil fuels and*

other carbon intensive industries; conserving biodiversity by leaving the ecological integrity of natural ecosystems unharmed and scaling up ecological restoration; transforming industrial agriculture towards agroecological practices; and investing in electrified, free or subsidized mass public transit. There are more real solutions than false ones. ●

If you watched David Attenborough's beautifully made and Netflix produced witness statement "A life on our planet," you may have come away with the idea that desert renewable technology can save us. Yet, the world is embroiled in an energy contradiction. Hundreds of millions of people around the world are unable to access energy to carry out basic functions - such as heating their homes and powering cooking appliances - while multinational corporations are ramping up land-grabs in the name of energy provision for a tiny minority of the global population. Whether for export oriented and mass produced food, or energy (however green) these land grabs must end.

13% of the world's population have no access to electricity, and 40% do not have access to clean fuel both of which have severe impacts for health, education and wellbeing. Almost all of the people in both these are located in the Global South.[27] The International Energy Agency (IEA) estimates that the annual cost of reaching the goal of universal energy access will be around USD$48 billion by 2030. In comparison, the International Finance Corporation (IFC) indicates that those without access to modern energy services spend USD$37 billion per year globally on low-quality cooking and lighting energy. The global poor spend three to ten times more of their disposable income on energy than the rich.

Indeed, the poor are already spending nearly as much on fuels as would be required in capital investment to provide accessible renewable energy (which has high upfront costs but very low operating costs).[28] The costs of addressing the health consequences of household air pollution from unventilated cooking with fuelwood and charcoal (which contribute to asthma, acute respiratory infections, tuberculosis, strokes, low birth weight, and cataracts, among other healthcare risks)[29] means that it would be cheaper - and more dignified - to

27 Ritchie, Hannah and Max Roser (2019). 'Access to Energy.' Oxford Martin School, University of Oxford.

28 ILO (2013). 'Providing clean energy and energy access through cooperatives.' ILO.

29 Applied Research Programme on Energy and Economic Growth (2016). "Energy in Nepal". Applied Research Programme on Energy and Economic Growth

invest in universal clean energy access rather than relying on an already failed market driven approach. In the Global North, private energy companies are reaping record high profits whilst the elderly and working classes experience severe health impacts from being unable to afford increasingly extortionate energy bills. In the UK, one person dies every seven minutes from the cold.[30]

Land grabs have historically been the bread and butter of the fossil fuel industry. However, as the climate crisis creates pressure to transition to a post-carbon world, 'green' does not always equal 'good' when it comes to community-driven land sovereignty.[31] Across Latin America, South East Asia and Africa, efforts to attain energy efficiency and develop large-scale biofuel development have led to land-grabbing by both local and foreign entities - farmers whose land is seized by multinational corporations are left without an income, and forced to buy the commodities they once grew.[32] Proposals to cover the Western Sahara in solar panels assumes empty open space available for exploitation by European and US companies who will generate profitable renewable sources of energy for consumption in the Global North. Israel's reputation as a 'hub' for solar energy is built on the commercial solar fields in the occupied West Bank, while Palestinians remain unable to access consistent energy supplies.[33]

Alternative systems of energy generation - grounded in principles of decentralised, democratic and public energy ownership - is entirely possible in today's technological context.[34] We could all have solar panels on our homes and wind and tidal energy in our local communities. Libraries, hospitals, museums, schools and universities could be built to generate more energy than they consume. We could collectively contribute to the generation of green energy, and participate in decision making about how to allocate it - specifically towards socially valuable activities (to limit the extractivism required for green infrastructure). Only by moving away from a model that privileges the enrichment of oligarchal energy companies can we have the space to develop a renewable energy system in harmony with principles of land sovereignty

30 Foster, Dawn (2016). 'Why is one older person dying every seven minutes during the winter?'. The Guardian.

31 Borras Jr, Santurnino and Jennifer C. Franco (2012). 'A 'Land Sovereignty' Alternative: Towards a Peoples' Counter-Enclosure'. TNI.

32 GRAIN (2013). 'Land grabbing for biofuels must stop'. GRAIN.

33 Who Profits (2017). 'Greenwashing the Occupation: The Solar Energy Industry and the Israeli Occupation'. Who Profits.

34 Steinfort, Lavinia (2019). 'The Future is Public: Democrratic energy economies can avert climate catastrophe'. TNI.

and energy security.[35] It is crucial that the zero-carbon world envisioned in progressive Green New Deals is not used as cover for a new generation of 'green' colonialism, and instead deepens energy democracy with universal and sustainable access that supports the well-being of all.

Green Energy Grabs
HAMZA HAMOUCHENE

Hamza Hamouchene is the North Africa Programme Coordinator at the Transnational Institute based in London, UK.

In this context where the energy security of the North trumps the human rights and sovereignty of people in the south, where priorities are dictated by the richest and most powerful (states and multinationals), it is of paramount importance to scrutinise the political economy of energy transitions.

Two examples of renewable energy schemes in North Africa show how energy colonialism is reproduced in the form of green colonialism or green grabbing.

The Ouarzazate Solar Plan was launched in 2016 just before the Marrakech climate talks (COP22). It was praised as the largest solar plant in the world and the Moroccan monarchy was declared a champion of renewable energies. The plant was installed on Amazigh agro-pastoralist communities' land without their approval and consent, a land grab for a supposedly green agenda (a green grab). Second, this mega-project is controlled by private interests and has been built through contracting a huge debt of USD$9 billion from the World Bank, European Investment Bank, and others. This debt is

35 Friends of the Earth et al. (2018). 'Energy Cities, "Unleashing The Power Of Community Renewable Energy'. Friends of the Earth.

backed by Moroccan government guarantees, which means potentially more public debts for a country already overburdened. Third, the project is not as green as it professes. It is using concentrated thermal power (CSP) that necessitates extensive use of water in order to cool down and clean the panels. In a semi-arid region like Ouarzazate, diverting water use from drinking and agriculture is outrageous.[36]

Similarly the Tunur Solar project in Tunisia highlights how patented green technology is extracted while locals struggle to have access to sufficient energy to meet their basic needs. A private venture between British, Maltese and Tunisian entrepreneurs, it aims to develop low cost dispatchable power to Europe. A familiar colonial scheme is being rolled in front of our eyes: the unrestricted flow of cheap natural resources (including solar energy) from the Global South to the rich North while fortress Europe builds walls and fences to prevent human beings - who seek dignified lives - from reaching safe shores.

We must always ask the relevant questions: who owns what? Who does what? Who gets what? Who wins and who loses? And whose interests are being served?

To implement just and truly green new deals, which provide for the future of people and planet, we must take nature back from the clutches of big capital and recast the debate around justice, popular sovereignty of the masses and collective good. The priority must be energy autonomy for local communities and a radical democracy that takes precedence over the logic of a market that considers our land and our livelihoods as commodities to be sold to the highest bidders. ●

---

36 Hamouchene, Hamza (2016). 'The Ouarzazate Solar Plant in Morocco: Triumphal 'Green' Capitalism and the Privatization of Nature'. Jadaliyya.

Can Land as a Carbon sink save us all?
KIRTANA CHANDRASEKARAN

Kirtana Chandrasekaran works for Friends of the Earth
International, based in Edinburgh, Scotland

Land based climate mitigation and adaptation is fast becoming a central theme in the response to the climate crisis. Corporations and Governments are hoping land can sequester millions of tonnes of carbon, to offset[37] their still rising emissions and help us reach 'net zero'[38] climate targets. The UK Committee on Climate change suggested last year 40% of the UK's mitigation targets could be met by carbon sequestration or so called 'negative emissions technologies' (NETs).[39] Shell, ENI and Heathrow airport have all made big commitments to achieving net zero via land based carbon offsets. This increasing reliance on carbon sequestration is itself a result of the major failure of industrialised country Governments for over 3 decades to put in place the structural changes needed to reduce emissions in all sectors - fossil fuels and the industrial food system which contributes anywhere between 30 – 50% of GHGs with its huge fertilizer use, contribution to deforestation and international trade.[40]

Carbon offsets are a major red herring, but even just the large scale use of land for climate mitigation can be problematic. How land is used, by whom and for what purpose are deeply political, not technical issues that movements for food sovereignty and land justice especially in the global south have been grappling with for decades. These movements have made important gains in getting recognition of their collective rights to land and territories via international Human Rights

---

37 'Carbon offsets claim to compensate for the emission of carbon dioxide via other activities such as planting trees. In reality, this allows the buyer's emissions to continue, instead of requiring them to cut their emissions at source.

38 The basic concept of "net zero" can be captured in an equation: greenhouse gas emissions minus carbon drawdown equals zero.

39 "The IPCC's climate change report: "Negative emissions" and business as usual" Redd Monitor October 2018

40 "Food sovereignty: five steps to cool the planet and feed its people" GRAIN, 2014.

instruments such as the UN Declaration on the Right of Peasants, UN Declaration on the Rights of Indigenous Peoples and historical agreements such as the International Conference on Agrarian Reform. But now land based climate policies imposed from above can pose grave threats to these rights by unleashing a new wave of land grabbing through enclosures for conservation projects but also via the commodification and integration of nature into financial markets – what we call the financialization of nature.[41]

Almost all of the plans for 'net zero' not only deflect action further but also require eye watering areas of land. Estimates of the land required globally to deploy bioenergy with carbon capture and storage (BECCS) range from 100 to 3000 million hectares.[42] Even the more benign sounding 'Nature Based Solutions' for climate change estimate 14 million hectares of destructive monoculture tree plantations and a whopping 678 million hectares of land for reforestation.[43] It's not clear who will claim ownership of these areas of land or where they will come from, but we can guess based on recent announcements by fossil fuel corporations. ENI, is involved in a gas extraction project in Mozambique and has been implicated in kicking 550 families off their land and blocking fisherfolk from the sea. At the same time ENI has committed to planting 20 million hectares of forest in Africa to achieve net zero by 2030. For the communities living on the land and forest this is essentially a double land grab – once for gas extraction and again to offset it.

On the other hand decentralised solutions to the climate crisis based on ecological, autonomous management, traditional knowledge and governance by Indigenous people, forest peoples, small scale food producers of their own land and territories such as agroecology and community forest management (CFM) already exist and are gaining importance.[44][45] CFM is the best way to protect forests and ecosystems

---

41 Regulated Destruction, FoEI 2019.

42 "The risks of relying on tomorrow's 'negative emissions' to guide today's mitigation action" Stockholm Environment Institute 2016

43 Griscom et al, 2017

44 "Agroecological and other innovative approaches for sustainable agriculture and food systems that enhance food security and nutrition" HLPE, CFS July 2019

45 "Community Forest Management - An opportunity to preserve and restore vital resources for the Good Living of human societies" FoEI, April 2018

that naturally store carbon, and agroecology can reduce the use of fossil fuels, increase yields and store carbon in soils. We just need political will to support them and scale them up. Many of the worlds 600 million peasants and over a billion forest dependant people have practiced agroecology and CFM for millenia. Yet many of the most prominent environmental schemes do not envision decentralised solutions with truly local autonomy and governance or justice but aim to keep the status quo in power relations and may even enable corporations to grab more natural resources.

If a green new deal is to succeed it must go beyond a Northern mindset and learn from historical movements in the global south. It must recognise that the link between the climate crisis and land rights are not new. The structural causes of the climate crises and land rights violations are the same – an economic system based on endless (neo) colonial patterns of natural resource extraction and accumulation[46]. Communities on the land – peasants, indigenous peoples, pastoralists, fishers especially women have always been the first line of defence against extractive projects and climate change. This is why mining corporations and agribusiness are the sectors most responsible for the documented killings of land and environmental Human Rights defenders.[47] If we want to succeed in building a world for climate justice keeping peoples on the land is our responsibility. ●

46 Summary for policy makers of the global assessment report on biodiversity and ecosystem services, Intergovernmental Science-Policy Platform on Biodiversity and Ecosystem Services May 2019

47 "At What Cost? Irresponsible business and the murder of land and environmental defenders in 2017" Global Witness July 2018

Illustration by Molly Crabapple

6. BLUE NEW DEAL: WATER, ICE AND OCEANS

As the health of our soil and air depletes, so does that of our rivers, glaciers and oceans. The IPCC's September 2019 special report on The Ocean and Cryosphere in a Changing Climate concluded that warming oceans, melting ice, and rising sea levels are already affecting everything from coral reefs to the nearly 10% of the global population living in low-lying coastal areas, and that negative impacts will greatly worsen in the future.[1]

As ice melts in the Himalayas, Andes, New Zealand, Rockies, Southern Alps, as well as in the Arctic and Antarctic, unique ecosystems are endangered and local communities face food and water stress. Glacial outburst floods pose risk to downstream communities and infrastructure - such outbreak floods from three lakes in the Bolivian Ande alone (Pelechuco lake, Laguna Arkhata and Laguna Glaciar) could expose 800-2100 people to life threatening floods.[2] Glacial retreat is also impacting food sustainability where agricultural irrigation systems are fed by glaciers and snowmelt. While glacial melt will initially increase water flow into rivers (sometimes causing floods) the ice is disappearing and in South Asia, a future water crisis looms for 270

---

1   IPCC (2019). 'Special Report on the Ocean and Cryosphere in a Changing Climate'. IPCC.

2   Kougkoulos, Ioannis et al. (2018). 'Modelling glacial lake outburst flood impacts in the Bolivian Andes'. Natural Hazards.

million people as Himalayan glaciers shrink.[3] Along with melting ice, the expansion of ocean waters as a result of temperature increases is driving rapid sea level rise. This in turn, causes displacement in low-lying islands, as well as crop failure from salt water intrusions of groundwater supplies in places like Bangladesh and Senegal.

Warming oceans also threaten the survival of marine life and ocean ecosystems. Even if global warming is limited to the agreed target of 1.5°C, it is projected that up to 90% of warm water coral reefs will be lost.[4] This loss is also down to the fact that since 1955, more than 90 percent of the energy trapped by the atmosphere as a result of increased greenhouse gases has been absorbed into the oceans. The resulting ocean acidification is bleaching coral reefs, which are some of the most biodiverse ecosystems in the world. Reefs provide critical food resources for tens of millions of people, but bleached coral is poisoning fish. Pacific Island nations, like Tuvalu and Vanuatu, are already experiencing these consequences of warming water - with increased flooding, erosion and extreme weather patterns. For a country like Vanuatu, despite only contributing 0.0016% of global carbon emissions, a single cyclone in 2015 wiped away more than half their GDP.[5] Two of Tuvalu's nine islands have already submerged - and the "sea is eating the sand" of the remaining islands. As the soil becomes saltier, farming crops in these lands becomes increasingly difficult.[6]

In Bangladesh, a combination of river erosion, flooding and storms are making it difficult for local communities to farm wheat, chillies, pulses, nuts and more. Many farmers are pushed into day-labouring in informal precarious work. Those that can afford to travel move to the capital city - with more than 1300 individuals estimated to move from rural parts of Bangladesh to Dhaka every year. These migrations tend to be due to the immediate impacts of a disaster, or due to slow-onset climate impacts such as salt water intrusion or reduced fish stocks.[7]

Similarly, 6000 inhabitants of low-lying islands in Melanesia are being forced from their homes and made stateless as a result of rising sea levels and

3 Albinia, Alice (2020). 'A water crisis looms for 270 million people as South Asia's glaciers shrink.' National Geographic.

4 IPCC (2018). 'Special Report: Global Warming of 1.5°C: Summary For Policymakers.' IPCC.

5 GFDRR (2018). 'Weathering financial shocks from disasters in the Pacific Islands.' GFDRR.

6 Pasley, James (2020). 'The Pacific Islands are drowning under rising sea levels. These stunning photos show their precarious way of life.' Business Insider.

7 Mulder, Natasha (2019). 'Surviving climate change and migration in Bangladesh.' ActionAid.

saltwater inundation[8] - this includes the displacement of the entire population of the Carteret Islands.[9] This loss of connections to ancestral lands where families are buried and traditional ways of life are pursued, where a common language is expressed, and a particular way of participating in democratic life is enacted will be unrepairable. The relocation of climate refugees from the Carteret Islands has been left to an NGO called Tulele Peisa, formed by local elders in response to central government inaction. Tulele Peisa managed to secure 0.81 square kilometres, a gift of four abandoned plantations from the Catholic Church of the nearby Bougainville island - but it still needs another 14 square kilometres. As of 2018, Tulele Peisa had built eight houses on Bougainville Island, and rehabilitated 14 family parcels with cocoa and coconut trees.[10]

In Senegal, lands that were previously abundant have not been harvested for decades. Fish, oysters and other sea life is diminishing, causing food insecurity. Waterside mangrove trees are the breeding grounds for fish and shellfish, but depend on a delicate balance of brackish water - which mixes freshwater from the river with salt water from the sea. But as rainfall reduces upstream and sea levels have risen, the freshwater component has reduced and river saltwater levels have increased. Mangroves die and leave vast infertile mudflats, so gathering oysters and other shellfish has become much harder, thereby hitting the river fishing and shellfish economy.[11] Mangroves are also significant natural flood defenses and absorb carbon.[12] In September 2019, 4,000 people were displaced after flooding in Senegal.[13]

The average person in Papua New Guinea, Bangladesh, or Senegal emits 0.4 - 0.9 metric tonnes of CO_2 per year, compared to Australia, which has an average per capita footprint of 17 tonnes, followed by the US at 16.2 tonnes, and Canada at 15.6 tonnes.[14] These figures do not include the carbon embedded in the products that people in the Global North consume, but which

8   Blitz, Brad K. (2011). 'Statelessness and Environmental-Induced Displacement: Future Scenarios of Deterritorialization, Rescue and Recovering Examined.' Mobilities 6(3), p.433-450.

9   Connell, John (2016). 'Last days in the Carteret Islands? Climate change, livelihoods and migration on coral atolls.' Asia Pacific Viewpoint 57(1), p.3-15.

10 Munoz, Sarah (2019). 'Understanding the human side of climate change relocation.' The Conversation.

11 ActionAid (2015). 'On the Edge: Climate Impacts and Adaptation in West Africa.' ActionAid.

12 Dia Ibrahima, M (2012). 'Vulnerability Assessment of Central Coast Senegal (Saloum) and The Gambia Marine Coast and Estuary to Climate Change Induced Effects.' Coastal Resources Centre and WWF-WAMPO, University of Rhode Island.

13 Floodlist News (2019). 'Senegal - Thousands Displaced by Floods in Dakar and Kaolack Regions.' Floodlist.

14 Ritchie, Hannah (2019). 'Where in the world do people emit the most CO2?.' Our World in Data, University of Oxford.

are made elsewhere (predominantly in the Global South) and transported by carbon heavy freight or air. Frontline climate change impacts are not felt in the countries most responsible historically, and the countries where per capita greenhouse gas emissions continue to be disproportionately high.

In addition to all this, as permafrost thaws and decomposes, it slowly releases thousands of years worth of carbon and methane that it holds, accelerating the greenhouse effect and increasing risks of long dormant bacteria and viruses reviving, making future pandemics more likely.[15]

It is in this context that our contributing authors consider what the blue in a globally just Green New Deal could look like. The values that are promoted throughout the pieces would see globally just Green New Deals underscore our interdependence with the natural world, rather than continuing to see it as a site of extraction and exploitation, as is encouraged by the World Bank and others.[16] The ocean, a huge site of carbon absorption, would have time to heal, giving our remaining ocean creatures the ability to rebuild. Globally just Green New Deals would also ensure that water is no longer diverted from communities to corporations for unsustainable products made in precarious working conditions,[17] ensuring the universal right and access to clean water. Furthermore, flood defenses would be funded by those most culpable, and the right to move would be protected and promoted.

Reckoning with the social impacts of glacial melts
SUNIL ACHARYA

Sunil Acharya is the Regional Advisor for Climate And Resilience Practical Action in Kathmandu, Nepal.

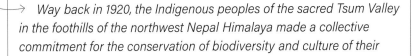

Way back in 1920, the Indigenous peoples of the sacred Tsum Valley in the foothills of the northwest Nepal Himalaya made a collective commitment for the conservation of biodiversity and culture of their

---

15 Fox-Skelly, Jasmin (2017). 'There are diseases hidden in ice, and they are waking up.' BBC Earth.

16 https://www.worldbank.org/en/news/infographic/2017/06/06/blue-economy; see also https://blogs.worldbank.org/endpovertyinsouthasia/investing-bhutans-forests-sustainable-future

17 See for example, https://waronwant.org/media/coca-cola-drinking-world-dry

local area for the benefit of the many generations to come.[18] The valley residents were gearing up for centennial celebrations to reaffirm and renew the commitments in a cultural festival to be organized in April 2020. They were forced to postpone the event until further notice due to Covid-19. While they have always remained the custodians of nature, a much greater threat looms large – the threat of climate change – with the prospect of displacing them and their culture entirely.

Around 1.9 billion people across the South Asian subcontinent depend upon Himalayan glaciers for drinking water, agriculture and energy. Due to climate change, these glaciers are melting twice as fast as they were in the year 2000.[19] Some parts of the Himalayan region are warming fast, three times faster than the global average. In 2019, a comprehensive climate change study focused on the Hindu Kush, Himalaya found that even if global collective action can contain the temperature rise to 1.5°C, at least one third of the Himalayan glaciers would melt by the end of this century. At the current rate of global greenhouse emission and warming, the Himalayas could lose two thirds of its glaciers by 2100.[20] Glacial lake outburst floods will wash away people and infrastructure in the mountain slopes with more frequent floods (in the already fragile region) until around 2050, increasing river discharge. In the longer term, we will see persistent droughts with glacier-less mountains and water-less rivers.

Scores of villages in the Himalayas have already been forced to relocate elsewhere due to scarcity of water. One example is residents of Dhye village in Mustang District of Nepal. The village people have historically adjusted their agriculture-based livelihood to an arid environment and have been balancing their material needs within nature's limits. However, climate change has rendered their livelihoods more difficult. The Dhye villagers were forced to relocate to a nearby area, Thanchung. The government calls this relocation illegal and encroachment of national property thus rendering Dhye villagers 'climate

18 Rai, J et al., (2016). 'Sacred Tsum Valley: Improving biodiversity conservation with lessons for effective management of protected areas in Nepal.' In Verschuuren, B and Furuta, N (eds). Asian Sacred Natural Sites: Philosophy and Practice in protected areas and conservation. Pp. 121-138. Routledge.

19 Maurer, J.M et al., (2019). 'Acceleration of ice loss across the Himalayas over the past 40 years.' ScienceAdvances.

20 Solly, Meilan (2019). 'The Himalayas could lose two-thirds of its glaciers by 2100.' Smithsonian Magazine.

refugees,' albeit displaced internally within Nepal.[21]

The Andes have also been impacted. Peru alone has lost up to 50 percent of its glacial ice in the past three to four decades. Glacial lake outburst floods have resulted in the loss of thousands of lives. In 1941, a single devastating flood from Lake Palcacocha killed more than five thousand people and destroyed the city of Huaraz. Climate change has made this deadly lake more dangerous for current and future generations.[22]

While the countries of these regions have made negligible contributions to climate change and resulting impacts, the dominant approach to development and its pathway is hastening the crisis. Governments, motivated by their development partners, build infrastructure in the Himalayan region without giving proper consideration to geological and environmental risks. In the rush for short term economic growth, hydropower promotes enrichment for the companies that own the dams with negative impacts to local communities many of whom live with energy poverty as the water generated energy is exported to other regions and countries. Over 20 million people in Nepal, 82 percent of the population, lack access to clean and safe methods of energy for cooking, disproportionately exposing the women who undertake this labour to toxic air. Household air pollution from unventilated cooking with fuelwood and charcoal presents a serious public health hazard,

21 Prasain, Suresh (2018). 'Climate change adaptation measure on agriculture communities of Dhyhe in Upper Mustang, Nepal'. Climatic Change 148(2).

22 Orlove, Ben (2017). 'Palcacocha icefalls demonstrate hazard vulnerabilities in Peru'. Phys Org.

Illustration by Tomekah George

contributing to asthma, acute respiratory infections, tuberculosis, strokes, low birth weight, and cataracts, among other healthcare risks.

Dams also displace and the majority of displaced people are indigenous communities who have made their homes in the mountains. Dams also increase the risk of earthquakes (in an already vulnerable region). A study conducted after the 2015 Nepal earthquake called for an urgent revaluation of hydropower development in the region. It reported that about 25 percent of hydropower projects are likely to be damaged by the landslides triggered by earthquakes.[23] Similarly, road projects across the Himalaya region pose threats to the fragile ecosystems. By-passing the required environmental assessments and management plans, they tear through pristine areas that have been protected by indigenous communities for hundreds of years. All these damages are mistakenly viewed as the necessary costs of development but these dominant views do not answer: for whose benefit is this development? What does development mean if it takes away so much? If development is the story of who we want to become, whose story is promoted while silencing others? What are we leaving for future generations?

While the climate crisis and current Covid-19 pandemic has exposed the thin margins on which the global economic order runs, and how it is devoid of the capacity to deal with shocks and uncertainties, it has also presented the opportunity to rethink how we address poverty, economic injustice and the climate crisis. One framework that is creating a vision to build a healthier, more resilient and sustainable future is the Green New Deal, propagated mostly from the industrial world. We need to examine the merit of these proposals from the perspective of the Global South. This framework alone cannot drive the fundamental systemic shifts required to transition away from our shared crises. Unless those on the frontline of disaster development, climate change and marginalisation are participating in discourses meaningfully, and leading our visions for alternative futures, we will forever make cosmetic changes to a system that has historical roots in exploitation, extraction and displacement. ●

23 Qiu, Jane (2018). 'Landslides pose threat to Himalayan hydropower dream.' Nature.

Ocean in our Blood: The Maori fight for water and against Empire
TINA NGATA

Tina Ngata is an Environmental, Indigenous And Human Rights Advocate based in Te Ika A Maui.

I am, as a Pacific Woman, a member of a water nation. I am an ocean person. In saying this, I mean I am the ocean, as a person. My layers of ancestry back to the ocean are recorded, and recountable, and each of those ancestors exist within me, including my ancestor ocean. Hence why we so readily say, in the Pacific:

"We sweat and cry salt water, so we know that the ocean is really in our blood."[24]

Water is therefore, from my Indigenous perspective, an issue of relationships. The severance of these relationships is one of the greatest open wounds of imperialism. Imperialism took my Indigenous ocean nation, sliced it up, and apportioned its control around the world. It is said that within the next decade, over 700 million people worldwide could be displaced through water scarcity.[25] Water, in my world, is the great connector, but in the hands of Empire, it is used to divide, displace, and impoverish.

Maori fight for water to have intrinsic rights because we understand it as an intelligent being. Water's intelligence is comprised of the multiple lifeforms within and around it, and the waterbody itself. To understand and respond adaptively to water therefore requires a localised relationship. Governing water from centralised imperial power hubs is the least effective model of water protection. For thousands of years, Indigenous peoples have kept our waters clean, life supporting, and abundant. In a short time, imperialism, in a multitude of forms, disrupted that.

24 Teaiwa, Teresia. (2017). 'We sweat and cry salt water, so we know that the ocean is really in our blood.' International Feminist Journal of Politics, 19(2), 133-136.

25 UN (2020). 'Water.' UN.

26 Roy, Arundhati. (2003). 'Confronting empire.' Sterneck.

We must therefore confront imperialism if we genuinely want to protect water. We must know imperialism's source, and we must know its extensions. We must understand its function not only in multinational corporations, but also in NGOs, in governments, and in the global institutions that service them. We must, as Arundhati Roy says, force empire into the open, we must make it drop its mask[26]. In the context of the Global Green New Deal, that is the mask of paternal benefaction which disguises a global power complex rooted in imperialist entitlement. Without such exposure, we will continue to fail climate commitments, Sustainable Development Goals, and the Global Green New Deal.

In my culture, polluted waters are a metaphor for a polluted mind. It is a polluted mind that tells me my Indigenous rights are inferior to imperial rights. It is a polluted mind that suggests the oppressed should appeal to the oppressor to grasp the Global Green New Deal. It is a polluted mind that suggests the enslaver will protect the interests of the slave. Either you, as an Imperialist oppressor and beneficiary, are interested in justice or you are not. You do not get to establish its parameters for your own gain and maintain the role of a humanitarian benefactor. The Global Green New Deal therefore demands a new global power infrastructure that is independent of the Imperialist behemoth, with full powers to hold that behemoth to account, and a true benefactor of humanity will champion that step. ●

Blue Imaginaries for a Green New Deal
JESSICA LEHMAN & ELIZABETH JOHNSON

Dr Jessica Lehman is Assistant Professor in the Department Of Geography at Durham University in Durham, UK; and Elizabeth Johnson is Professor in the Department Of Geography at Durham University in Durham, UK.

Marine scientists, environmental economists, and politicians have argued that a global green new deal should meaningfully include the ocean. Proposals for a 'blue new deal,' or a 'teal deal' would integrate land- and sea-based initiatives. Advocates of an oceanic new deal[27] indicate a number of areas where environmental sustainability and economic gain could be achieved, and "good paying, union jobs" created. These include emissions-cutting measures in marine transportation, sustainable fisheries management, aquaculture, and marine habitat protection.

There is much to like about a global blue new deal. As an interdisciplinary group of scientists, environmental economists, and geographers explained in Conservation Letters earlier this year, incorporating the ocean into visions of an environmentally stable future would first require a change in our ocean imaginary. Rather than viewing the oceans "as climate change aggressors (e.g., sea level rise) or victims (e.g., coral reef decline)" a 'teal deal' necessitates that we would first "recognize oceans as an integral part of climate solutions".[28] This focus on possibility rather than catastrophe is refreshing. Moreover, a blue new deal presents an opportunity to understand the oceans beyond binary terms as risky or at risk - and to see them as deeply connected to land-based human activities and social and economic value systems. And, the blue new deal focuses more astutely on issues of social justice and inequality than the recent spate of proposals, anchored in various nations, for the development of the 'blue economy.'

However, we want to flag three significant and related risks of a global blue (or teal) new deal as it has been discussed in political and environmental circles and as it manifests in associated ocean imaginaries. The first is linked to the discourses of global good that permeate blue new deal language. The high seas and their resources (as well as the resources of the international seabed) have been codified into international law as being for the benefit of "all mankind". The global ocean, its living inhabitants, and its nonliving resources are often viewed as just that: part of what the UN Convention on the Law of the Seas (UNCLOS) calls the "heritage of all mankind" and part of

27 Dundas, Steven J. et al., (2020). 'Integrating oceans into climate policy: Any green new deal needs a splash of blue.' Conservation Letters, 13(5).

28 Ibid

a global common. Thinking with the oceans and the interconnection between marine, terrestrial, and atmospheric matters encourages this viewpoint. Yet, these discourses do not simply elide the often complex, overlapping, and contradictory juridical regimes that shape global ocean governance (many of which are laid out in UNCLOS). They also are used as foils behind which space is held open for ocean resources to be exploited[29] by particular nations and global corporations (Zalik 2015).

Second, these blue and teal deal proposals also risk perpetuating an understanding of the oceans as a realm of untapped potential. Although the 'blue new deal' steps encouragingly away from notions of the ocean as a space for limitless and friction-free capital accumulation (for example by calling for the end of deep-sea drilling), there is the potential in these discourses to reproduce notions of the oceans as reservoirs of resources and services, even if these services include carbon sequestration and small-scale livelihood provision.

A third related concern is the trap of nostalgia that permeates much of the GND discourse. The original New Deal in the United States was intimately tied to the entrenchment of settler colonialism in the United States. This included the establishment of large-scale infrastructure projects as well as the continuation of the violence of Native American boarding schools,[30] which expanded throughout the 20th century. In the United Kingdom, proposals to catalyze a "Green Industrial Revolution" similarly bury the extractive violence that accompanied the first Industrial Revolution. Visions of the global ocean as a project for economic expansion risks the erasure, elision, and repetition of these colonial histories and ideologies.

Taken together, ignoring these risks would mean falling into a trap that sees the oceans as 'aqua nullius,' spaces of untapped potential resources (whether carbon sequestration potential or marine protein) and realms where current and historical relations between humans, and between humans and nonhumans, are secondary if acknowledged at all. In doing so, questions of who exactly benefits from such measures

29 Zalik, Anna (2015). 'Trading on the Offshore: Territorialization and the Ocean Grab in the International Seabed.' In Ervine, Kate and Gavin Fridell (Eds) Beyond Free Trade. International Political Economy Series. Palgrave Macmillan, 173-190.

30 Pember, Mary Annette (2019). 'Death by Civilization.' The Atlantic.

and whose lives will be potentially harmed by them are often left unaddressed. Moreover, other ways of valuing and relating to ocean space outside of a system of quantified accounting and economic exchange are left unexplored. Therefore, we argue that issues of marine governance and equality must be foregrounded in discussions of a blue new deal and must be approached with an analytic capable of accounting for the different imaginaries, value systems, and relationships with and of the ocean that proliferate around the world. In short, imagining a "teal deal" requires contending not with an imagined "global ocean" in the singular, but with overlapping and contested oceans in the plural.

The oceans have long been a space upon which utopian ideals, future possibilities, and even the salvation of humanity have been projected - by imperial powers and indigenous coastal communities alike. The oceans are an alluring and productive site for imagining otherwise. But a truly effective and equitable global blue new deal must be clear-eyed about the risks such imaginaries elide, and put issues of equality and justice-oriented governance first. ●

7. CLIMATE LINKED-MIGRATION: THE RIGHT TO MOVE AND THE RIGHT TO STAY

The aim of the climate justice movement must be that nobody is forcibly displaced from their home. Climate-induced displacement is often driven by people not having the resources to adapt to the consequences of climate change, being forced to adopt mal-adaptive policies, like industrial agriculture which depletes vulnerable resources which hasten the crisis, or - or suddenly evacuating in the face of a storm or flood without support to return. In some cases, it becomes inevitable in the absence of seawalls high enough or flood defenses strong enough. The removal of loan conditions that require austerity, the cancellation of debt and the provision of meaningful climate financing or reparations could fund universal access to social protection measures - making the choice to stay or move a genuine one. Such resources could also fund adaptation measures that increase resilience - this includes using scarce water resources more efficiently, adapting building codes to withstand new climate conditions and extreme weather events, building flood defences, investing in decent green jobs, and setting aside land corridors to help species migrate.

Illustration by Tomekah George

However, such defences cannot prevent the movement of those losing their islands or delta regions to rising seas. In the future, adaptation measures will not prevent movement from areas that have been made unfarmable or too hot for human survival. This reality requires a holistic approach to protecting both the right to stay and live a dignified life, as well as enshrining and protecting the right to move with dignity too.

According to UNOCHA, which co-ordinates the UN's humanitarian responses to emergencies, eight of the world's worst food crises are linked to both conflict and climate shocks.[1] Disasters have driven more than 70% of the 33.4 million newly displaced people that took place in 2019, with 23.9 million people displaced by weather related disasters (floods, storms, droughts, etc) alone.[2] Most of those who have been displaced live in Global South countries, who are collectively responsible for less than 4% of emissions. These

1 OCHA (2019). 'Global Humanitarian Overview 2020.' ReliefWeb.
2 IDMC (2020). 'Global Report on Internal Displacement 2020.' IDMC.

countries have not been equipped with the resources to support alternative forms of climate adaptation, and countries of the Global North, despite doing far more to cause climate change, have not provided the level of climate financing to resource infrastructures of resilience for countries on the frontline, instead they have often promoted industrialised agriculture and policies that increase exposure to climate impacts.

Climate-related displacement disproportionately impacts women and girls in Southern countries - in 2018, more than half of the 41 million people internally displaced were women.[3] Despite bearing the brunt of the impacts of climate crisis, Black and brown women in particular are excluded from the very decision making processes that have led to climate breakdown, as well as the policy decisions that determine how we respond to its consequences. Women and girls are also made more vulnerable by the impacts of climate-re-

3 Cazabat, Christelle (2020). 'Women and girls in internal displacement'. IDMC.

lated displacement for multiple reasons. As they tend to have greater care responsibilities, it is harder for them to leave home - and if they choose to leave, the process of migrating is fraught with risks of gender-based violence, such as trafficking or sexual assault. These risks remain high for those who have managed to migrate, especially for those who end up in informal settlements or displacement camps. Women and girls in lower-income countries are also driven to migrate because they tend to rely most on subsistence farming as an income source and food source, which often becomes scarce due to climate change.

Organizations like CARE International have developed some preliminary suggestions for how a global infrastructure of protection and support for those displaced by climate change could work. This includes ending what they call the "legal vacuum", which leaves those displaced by climate breakdown in a "legal No Man's land".[4] One way this could be done, is by ensuring countries that have historically done the most to cause climate breakdown, yet are cushioned from its worst impacts, open their borders and provide safe and legal means to citizenship for displaced people. This requires an active and persistent global migrants' rights movement fighting for the free and safe movement of people. Existing legal frameworks are not yet responsive to the particular struggles of climate-displaced people, especially as it intersects with gender inequality and oppression. Movements and policymakers attuned to this issue must therefore expand their responses to include the accessible and resourced provision of services for those subject to gender-based violence in all its forms. These social, political, legal and economic infrastructures of support for those who have to leave their homes because of climate-related issues must be financed and resourced in a way that is reparative and just. This means countries in the Global North paying their fair share, and fighting the tide of right-wing populism that responds to displaced people with borders, fences and racialized violence.

In the following piece, Jessica Faleiro outlines an example of how communities displaced by climate change are left unprotected and vulnerable to other crises - such as Covid-19.

---

4 CARE (2020). 'Evicted by climate change: Confronting the gendered impacts of climate-induced displacement.' CARE International.

Intersecting crises: a case study of climate migration in India in the wake of Covid-19.
JESSICA FALEIRO

Jessica Faleiro is the Project Lead of Actionaid International's South Asia And Climate (Samac) Project, based in Johannesburg, South Africa.

Climate change is driving forced displacement in India

According to the Global Report on Internal Displacement (GRID) 2020, India had the highest figure in the world of new internal displacements due to disasters in 2019. These 5 million displacements were caused by 'a combination of increasing hazard intensity, high population exposure and high levels of social and economic vulnerability.' The country also noted the seventh warmest year on record since 1901, and the wettest monsoon season in 25 years.[5] As a large country spread across many climatological and ecological zones, India is vulnerable to many different kinds of climate impacts including droughts, heat waves, flooding, rising sea levels and cyclones. However, the most vulnerable are the rural populations who are dependent on climate-sensitive livelihoods such as agriculture, fisheries or forestry. 67% of India's 1.3 billion people live in rural areas and still rely heavily on these sectors for their income.[6]

In 2016 a joint report by ActionAid, Bread for the World and Climate Action Network South Asia, noted that crop failure resulting from increasingly erratic rainfall or drought, and destruction of fishing livelihoods due to higher saline intrusion from rising sea levels forced people to migrate in search of work. As the study also noted: there is "a lack of data mapping of the role of climate change in overall migration trends in South Asia and its contribution is not yet clearly understood

---

5   IDMC (2020). 'India.' IDMC.

6   Anderson, T. et al., (2016). 'Climate change knows no borders: an analysis of climate induced migration, protection gaps and need for solidarity in South Asia.' ActionAid.

by policy makers. Even though climate change is clearly leading to ever-greater migration in the region, the lack of clear data and policy analysis means that the issue is still largely invisible in migration discourse and response."[7]

The impact on rural and migrant workers

According to India's 2011 Census data (the latest available) there are 17.8 million interstate and intrastate migrant labourers.[8] It is difficult to get data on what percentage of these labourers migrated specifically because of climate change related factors - however it is clear that people move when in need of income they cannot get locally.[9]

Climate change is often a key, exacerbating factor in the destruction of local income-generating activities - especially for rural communities. In 2017, the National Institute of Rural Development and Panchayati Raj, Hyderabad, reported that mass migration out of the hill areas of Uttarakhand had left behind several 'ghost villages' with nothing but barren fields and ruined houses as evidence that someone had once lived there.[10] The report of the state's Rural Development and Migration Commission, released in 2018, said that more than 70% of migration occurs within the state, indicating the movement of people from the state's hill regions to its plains.[11] There is a large difference in the soil fertility and agricultural development of the plains in comparison to the hill areas. Additionally, there is better industrial, transport and general infrastructure in place in the plains, allowing it to sustain a dense population. It is understandable as to why people would feel compelled to move from a place that lacks proper facilities and basic services, and where agriculture is difficult to sustain.

7 Ibid

8 Kundu, Sridhar (2020). 'At least 23 million migrants are returning to India's villages. Can the rural economy keep up?'. Scroll.in.

9 Anderson, T. et al., (2016). 'Climate change knows no borders: an analysis of climate induced migration, protection gaps and need for solidarity in South Asia'. ActionAid.

10 Mamgain, R.P., and Reddy, D.N. (2017). 'Outmigration from Hill Region of Uttarakhand: Magnitude, Challenges and Policy Options'. Rural Labour Mobility in Times of Structural transformation, p.209-235.

11 Rural Development and Migration Commission (2018). 'Interim Report on the Status of Migration in Gram Panchayats of Uttarakhand'. Rural Development and Migration Commission, Uttarakhand, Pauri Garhwal.

According to Uttarakhand's Action Plan on Climate Change:
"Climate change–driven fluctuations in the precipitation pattern have
increased uncertainty in the farm output and recurring crop failures
have left little incentive for the masses to continue with the same.
Labour-intensive hill farming has thus been rendered unsustainable
and the region is presently threatened by food insecurity. The repercus-
sions of this are clearly reflected in large stretches of hitherto regularly
sown agricultural lands being left barren. Climate change is thus taking
its toll on hill farming, agricultural diversity and the overall well-being of
the people". [12]

Displaced communities left vulnerable to Covid-19

Considering the sheer numbers of migrant labourers at interstate
and intrastate level, and the lack of data mapping, it isn't surprising that
when the government ordered a nation-wide Coronavirus lockdown
with only a few hours' notice on 24th March 2020, it was unprepared to
anticipate the scale of movement of internal migrants from urban areas
back to the villages they came from.

Soon after the lockdown was announced, large numbers of migrants
clustered around train and bus stations, anxious to return home when
they heard rumours that transport services might be running after
all. This was not the case, and hundreds of thousands of suddenly
unemployed migrants found themselves on the streets without food
or housing. Desperate and unable to observe social distancing, many
walked hundreds of kilometres back to the villages they'd left due to
climate change impacts. Many did not survive.

Shelters were set up in school buildings to house hundreds of
migrants at a time. Some were farmers who worked as seasonal
labourers, and couldn't get back to their villages to tend fields in
time for planting season, leading to further losses in income. Without
employment, most of these migrants are now dependent on food
handouts from state governments or charities to survive. Some have

---

12 Government of Uttarakhand (2014). 'Uttarakhand Action Plan on Climate Change: Transforming Crisis into Opportunity'. Government of Uttarakhand.

resorted to begging and sleeping rough. It took several months for trains to transport 6 million people back to their home states.[13]

In the midst of a mismanaged lockdown, tropical cyclone Amphan made landfall in West Bengal on 20 May 2020. Trees were uprooted, houses destroyed and electric and telephone towers severely damaged. Power outages lasted days. The state administration struggled to cope with the massive impact of Amphan as 800,000 people were forced into flood shelters, without any chance of social distancing for days. Many of the shelters were already housing several migrant workers who had returned to their state in the first week of May and were under quarantine.

In the case of Uttarakhand, reverse migration has gradually re-populated 550 'ghost villages' as migrants who had lost even long-term jobs returned to the villages they'd left to tend once-abandoned lands. This puts pressure on the government to provide basic access to proper health and education services,the absence of which, exacerbated by water scarcity, drove them to leave in the first place. The impact of the lockdown has only highlighted the lack of social protection for India's rural poor, which continues to go largely unaddressed in policy circles. ●

Tetet Lauron from the Phillipine climate movement addresses how climate crisis disproportionately impacts women, and proposes some key policy aims for a feminist and decolonial Global Green New Deal.

13 Special Correspondent (2020). '60 lakh migrants took 4,450 Shramik specials to reach their home states.' The Hindu.

Climate migration is a feminist issue
TETET LAURON

Tetet Nera-Lauron is a an Advisor at Rosa-Luxemburg-Stiftung, based in Manila, Philippines.

Climate change continues to exact a toll on people's lives, livelihoods and communities with weather-related disasters becoming more frequent and intense. Almost 25 million people have been displaced last year alone by 1,900 disasters spanning 140 countries and territories, the highest figure recorded since 2012.[14] That equates to roughly one person being displaced every second. These risks are increasing, and climate change is an added layer to the multiple vulnerabilities already faced by people of varying genders, races, sexualities and ages.

Climate-induced displacement is not gender neutral.[15] Women in all their diversities are disproportionately affected due to existing structural and systemic inequalities. 6 out of 10 of the poorest people in the world are women. They bear the brunt of unpaid care work, and earn less than men for work of equal value. And despite many advances on gender equality initiatives globally, many disparities remain both in developing and developed countries because of ingrained government policies, economic constraints and social norms.[16] Women continue to have limited access to resources, rights, mobility, and their voices are muted in shaping decisions and influencing policy.

Women are hit by a triple whammy when disasters strike. Already poor and marginalized, more women than men lose their lives not due to physical differences but to social and traditional constructs such as restrictive clothing, being the designated caregiver in the family, or restrained mobility without the company of a male relative. These constructs limit women's abilities to protect themselves in the aftermath of disasters. While seeking refuge in 'safer' ground,they face many

14 IDMC (2020). 'Global Report on Internal Displacement 2020'. IDMC.

15 Shreejaya, Shradha (2019). 'A study on the gender and social impacts of climate migration'. Rosa Luxemburg Stiftung.

16 UN Women (2018). 'Facts and Figures: Economic Empowerment'. UN Women.

other inequalities in accessing their fundamental human rights, social protection, and face systemic gender-based violence such as trafficking and other forms of bonded labour.

Proposals that aim to spur systemic transformations in the economy and environment in some of the world's richest but heavily polluting countries through Green New Deal (GND) are capturing the imagination of many the world over. But for any GND to be truly relevant, it must commit to changing the rules of the game not just within rich countries' own borders, but must extend to correcting the injustices of centuries of colonial plunder. This also includes the continuing models of ecological colonialism, with unfair trade and investment agreements resulting in greater poverty and underdevelopment in the Global South.

A decolonial, feminist global Green New Deal must actively interrogate and resist racial, gender, class, caste and sexuality hierarchies.[17] It must address the root causes of poverty and marginalization that results in the exclusion and multi-layered vulnerabilities of farmers, workers, fisherfolk, indigenous, migrants, half of which are women. The following are some key considerations to ensure this transformation is pro-migrant, pro-poor and pro-women:

- *Decolonize the international trade, investments and financial architecture and redress ecological colonialism. A GND must commit to limit and redistribute wealth, including the establishment of a multilateral debt restructuring framework to counter the global debt crisis, address tax evasion and illicit financial flows that drain the South of resources critical for the provision of public goods.*
- *Advance the longstanding call for climate debt or reparations from developed countries to compensate for emitting the vast majority of historical carbon emissions, as well as for the loss and damage incurred by ecological harm over centuries.*
- *Move to create care economies that deliver on human, economic and social rights.*

---

17 Women's Working Group on Financing for Development (2020). 'Feminists want system change, not climate change.' YouTube.

> • *Recognize that there is a right to move and a right to stay. No matter what the options are, fundamental human rights must be upheld and protected.*
>
> *As feminist climate justice advocates, we must engage in inter-sectional advocacy towards justice. Neoliberalism and capitalism will always be at odds with this vision. But we will also not give up on our beautiful planet and will work hard to create regenerative and care economies.* ●

Todd Miller and Alejandro Gonzalez explore how climate change is fueling the rise of right-wing populism. He looks at how increasingly draconian immigration policy in the US both impacts and is driven by the conditions of climate-displaced migrants in Central America.

Securitizing the crisis: Climate policy at the U.S. border
TODD MILLER

Todd Miller is an Independent Journalist based in Tucson, Arizona.

> *When sixteen year old Juan de Leon Gutiérrez left Tizamarte, Guatemala to go to the United States in April 2019, the drought had already set in. The coffee plants were dying where he had worked in the fields for $3 per day. The family was rationing and only eating one meal per day. He had told his mother Transito Gutiérrez: "Mommy I am going to cross over the border and I will send you money. It may not be every day, but I will when I can." [18]*
> *Even so, Transito didn't want her teenage son to go to the US where Juan was hoping to join his brother. Hardship and even death had long*

18 Abbott, Jeff (2019). "I lost my son': Guatemala mum mourns boy who died in US custody." Al Jazeera.

been part of Washington's deterrence strategy on its southern border. And, as more people are being displaced in Central America on a heating globe, US border policy is quickly becoming its climate policy.

Juan was not alone. Between 2017 and 2019, twelve other families facing similar circumstances had departed Tizamarte for the US. And the intensifying droughts in Tizamarte was but a microcosm of a larger Central American problem. An area known as 'the dry corridor', which extends over Guatemala, Honduras, El Salvador and beyond, has left 1.4 million people at risk of hunger due to a combination of drought and torrential rain and floods.   Eight in ten households were resorting to "crisis coping mechanisms," according to the World Food Programme (WFP).[19] More than 25% could not afford a basic market food basket, and 30% of those who have migrated from the dry corridor cited weather as their main reason.

As climate scientist Chris Castro put it: In Central America "the wet gets wetter, the dry gets drier, the rich get richer, the poor get poorer. Everything gets more extreme." [20]

The term "catastrophic convergence," coined by sociologist Christian Parenti in his book Tropic of Chaos: Climate Change and the New Geography of Violence, frames well what Castro was describing. As in many places around the world, today's ecological disruption exacerbates already-existing and long-standing economic and political crises that have already pushed people to the furthest brink.

In Guatemala the catastrophic convergence is vivid. The country has long had a system more beholden to economic oligarchies (both multinational corporate and local elite), and its structural political and economic precarity can be traced in many ways to the United States. Since 1900, the United States has blasted the atmosphere with 700 times[21] more carbon emissions than Guatemala, El Salvador, and Honduras combined. With so many factors at hand, it is difficult to parse out exactly how many people are on the move due specifically to climate change. However it is estimated that as many as one in three

19 UN World Food Programme (2019). 'Erratic weather patterns in the Central American Dry Corridor leave 1.4 million people in urgent need of food assistance'. UN.

20 Miller, Todd (2017). 'Central America: 'We're facing an unprecedented calamity''. Upside Down World.

21 DataBlog (2009). 'A history of CO2 emissions: How are 'emissions debts' influencing the Copenhagen negotiations?'. The Guardian.

people could be displaced for climate-related reasons across the globe by 2070, many from Central America.[22]

In this reality, the United States has built over the last 25 years a foreboding border apparatus. Countless billions of dollars have been spent on 700 miles of walls, surveillance technologies, and more than 20,000 armed Border Patrol agents, not to mention the US pressure, financing, and training of Mexican immigration, police, and military forces to patrol its southern border with Guatemala and Belize.[23]

The Department of Homeland Security has long been aware of the serious droughts inflicting the Central American/Guatemalan country-side and understands it as a driver to migration.[24]

But this awareness has not led to any discussion of a climate status, but rather a more long term strategy to prepare US borders for "mass migration." [25] *US border strategy has long been one of "deterrence" including the possibility that the crossing would put people in "mortal danger," as put in a 1994 Border Patrol strategy memo.*[26]

In Juan's case, that proved to be true.

When the US Border Patrol arrested him after crossing in early April, he was placed in a detention center for children. Two weeks later, he fell ill and died on April 29, one of many children who died in US custody in 2019.

"I lost my son," a devastated Transito told Al Jazeera. Unless something changes, this will continue to be the inevitable result of US climate policy in the 21st century. ●

22 Lustgarten, Abrahm (2020). 'The Great Climate Migration.' New York Times.

23 Miller, Todd (2014). 'Mexico: The US Border Patrol's newest hire.' Al Jazeera.

24 Soboroff, Jacob and Julia Ainsley (2019). 'Trump admin ignored its own evidence of climate change's impact on migration from Central America.' NBC News.

25 U.S. Department of Homeland Security (2013). 'DHS Climate Action Plan.' U.S. Department of Homeland Security.

26 US Border Patrol (1994). 'Border Patrol Strategic Plan: 1994 and Beyond.' DocumentCloud.

Climate change never comes alone
ALEJANDRO GONZÁLEZ

Alejandro González is a Researcher at Universidad Autónoma De Madrid in Madrid, Spain.

Irregular precipitation has made the Dry Corridor in Central America one of the most sensitive areas to climate change in the world. El Salvador, Honduras, Nicaragua and Guatemala are the most exposed to floods and droughts alike, and all fall within the top 20 countries affected by climate change. Between 2014 and 2019, these countries have witnessed losses of between 50 and 80% of crop yields, and farmers that produce basic grains are at greater risk of poverty or extreme poverty. Peasants used to rely on traditional knowledge for starting the cropping periods, but this is no longer feasible. Unpredictable weather conditions - such as the interruption of the wet season by dry period and the rise in floods - means loss of control over growing conditions.

With 60% of people in the Dry Corridor relying on subsistence agriculture, those who have had their crops ruined by long standing droughts now have to look for instant, short-term jobs on a daily basis in order to survive. Several reports have noticed a growing circulation of migrants within the Dry Corridor countries performing informal jobs. Women tend to migrate more than men to other countries, as they face restricted access to local land and few other working alternatives, while having to continue assuming care tasks.

The number of people having to migrate has increased across the world. For Central American families, this often looks like one family member migrating to the US, while the rest stay to care for the children and elderly. These roles have traditionally been shared between men and women - however, as climate hazards start to deplete the means of subsistence linked to land, and hostile immigration policies making border-crossing more perilous for women, migration to North America has become predominantly male. Even when relatives abroad manage to send stable remittances, marriages are not expected to be reunited anymore. Families are regularly broken apart - a story told by the infamous images of children detained at the US Southern border. ●

A just vision for climate migration
MARÍA FACIOLINCE & DANIEL MACMILLEN VOSKOBOYNIK

María Faciolince is the Power Shifts Project Lead at Oxfam, based in Barcelona, Spain; and Daniel Macmillen Voskoboynik is Co-Founder And Co-Editor at The World At 1C, based in Barcelona, Spain.

A world wracked by climate violence is a landscape of displacement. Rising seas shaving coastlines. Farmlands depleted by saltwater and extreme heat. Encroaching deserts. Coastal communities pummelled by cyclones. Ancestral territories deemed unlivable by extreme temperatures.

In eastern Africa, from Djibouti[27] to Mozambique[28], millions have been displaced by torrential rains, droughts, and cyclones. In the Pacific, where low-lying island nations are particularly vulnerable to sea level rise, preliminary research suggests[29] that people in over two-thirds of households in Tuvalu and Kiribati would consider migration as a response to environmental shocks. In Central Asia[30], environmental

27 Fagan, Laureen (2019). 'Africa's 'climate refugees are already here - and there'. Africa Times.

28 Wachiaya, Catherine (2020). 'One year on, people displaced by Cyclone Idai struggle to rebuild.' UNHCR UK.

29 UNU-EHS and UNESCAP (n.d.). 'Climate change and migration in the Pacific: Links, attitudes, and future scenarios in Nauru, Tuvalu, and Kiribati.' United Nations University.

30 Blondin, Suzy (2018). 'Environmental migrations in Central Asia: a multifaceted approach to the issue.' Central Asian Survey 38(2), p. 275-292.

transformations have been documented as strong contributory factors in the movement of millions.

In 2017, nearly 68.5 million people around the world were displaced - a third by extreme weather. From the World Bank to the United Nations, various institutions predict that between tens of millions to up to a billion people could be displaced by climate change within the next three decades.[31] But even these estimated figures are likely to be undercounts, given the often intricate ways in which climatic factors intertwine with others. In addition to being a direct driver of movement through intensified extreme weather events (typhoons, floods, forest fires), the slow violence of climate change is an injustice multiplier, accelerating other deprivations and drivers of movement.

So in a reality of escalating climate-induced migration, what do justice-centred approaches to displacement look like? One possible approach calls for an almost paradoxical double-right: the right to stay, and the right to move.

The right to stay

The opposite of displacement is emplacement: rooted connection within a territory, which requires the conditions necessary to reproduce life in it. Yet, increasing fragility driven by climate

31 Nature Climate Change (2019). 'From migration to mobility.' Nature Climate Change,9(895).

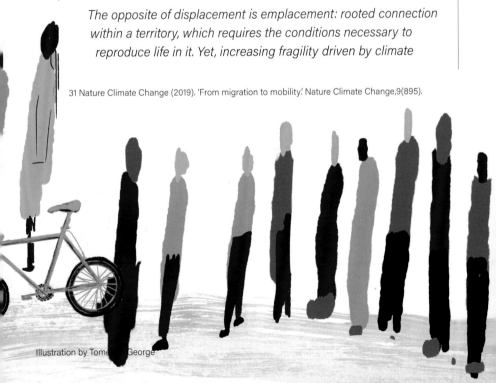

Illustration by Tomekah George

violence has led to many communities being displaced in situ.[32] Loss of place, and its life-giving environment, leaves communities stranded in their own territories without the ability to sustain their livelihoods.

Resettlement and migration are often forwarded as a mitigation strategy, but what social, economic and political protections are needed for communities to live with dignity in their own homes? Enshrining the right to stay involves everything to protect the rights of populations: from bold climate mitigation measures to ensure a safe climate, to strengthened land rights for indigenous communities and smallholder farmers, to active policies to support rural communities, to debt relief measures for the Global South, and gender-sensitive strategies to protect women and girls.

32 Feldman, Shelley and Charles Geisler (2011). 'Land grabbing in Bangladesh: In-situ displacement of peasant holdings.' Future Agricultures.

The right to move

But efforts to secure emplacement must live with the reality that significant displacement is underway and inevitable. Even with current levels of global heating, many territories are destined to be unlivable, if not already unlivable. The right to move is the right to have a pathway to safety, and mechanisms to rebuild a dignified life in a new territory.

The obstacles to 'the right to move' are numerous. Regimes of border imperialism, policing frontiers and criminalising those seeking to cross them in the hope of a better life, are being strengthened by the year. Displaced communities today meet the reality of detention, deportation and death, whether in the marine graveyards of the Mediterranean, or the dangerous crossings of the Darien Strait. Simply by extrapolating from the state of migrant rights protection today, we can easily envision a future of 'climate apartheid'.[33]

In addition, the architecture of protection for climate refugees is minimal, although some early cornerstones are emerging.[34] But even access to what is legally possible can be economically unrealistic. One study of rural communities in Malawi[35] found that 'climate change is likely to increase barriers to migration rather than increasing migration flows.' The aforementioned studies on attitudes towards migration across the Pacific found that the majority of people would not be able to afford the movement they deemed necessary.

The questions that remain

Climate displacement will stretch the contours of migration in unprecedented ways, and many questions remain. What kind of legal measures can protect the rights of those forced to uproot their lives by a systemic ecological crisis? How can protect 'new' rights in a context where existing protections for migrants and refugees are being so

---

33 UN Special Rapporteur on extreme poverty and human rights (2019). 'UN expert condemns failure to address impact of climate change on poverty.' UN OHCHR.

34 Mahecic, Andrej (2020). 'UN Human Rights Committee decision on climate change is a wake-up call, according to UNHCR.' UNHCR.

35 Suckall, N et al., (2017). 'Reduced migration under climate change: Evidence from Malawi using an aspirations and capabilities framework.' Climate and Development 9(4), p. 298-312.

swiftly eroded? How can we address the cultural-spiritual challenge of belonging in a landscape that is continuously degrading and changing? What is needed to face the challenge of changing demographic and social conditions in local communities receiving climate refugees, which in many cases are already facing significant climatic stress?[36] ●

36 McDonnell, Tim (2019). 'Climate change creates a new migration crisis for Bangladesh.' National Geographic.

Illustration by Molly Crabapple

8. FOREIGN POLICY

US and UK foreign policy has seen decades of systemic support for authoritarian oil and gas producers. In June 2019, the Court of Appeal (England & Wales) decided that Boris Johnson, Jeremy Hunt and Liam Fox and other key British ministers had illegally signed off on arms exports to Saudi Arabia without properly assessing the risk to civilians.[1] Since July 2020, the UK resumed arms sales to Saudi Arabia despite continued fears that the Saudi-led bombardment of Yemen has created the world's worst humanitarian crisis. The strategic value of oil was a key factor in the 2003 invasion of Iraq, and BP and Shell lobbied Tony Blair's government about their commercial opportunities in the country. The war – and preceding and subsequent conflicts in the region – cost hundreds of thousands of lives and destabilised the region. The military-industrial complexes of the West are also significant emitters of greenhouse gases[2] - the US Department of Defense is the world's biggest single consumer of commercial energy, consuming more than Nigeria, a country of almost 200 million.[3] In this way, the war economy presents a threat to human life in more ways than one.

Beyond seeking an immediate end of arms sales to fossil fuel producers, human rights abusing regimes and all parties involved in conflicts such as

---

1 Sabbagh, Dan and Bethan McKernan (2019). 'UK arms sales to Saudi Arabia unlawful, court of appeal declares.' The Guardian.

2 Wearing, David (2018). AngloArabia: Why Gulf Wealth Matters to Britain. Polity Press.

3 Crawford, Neta C. (2019). 'The Defense Department is worried about climate change - and also a huge carbon emitter.' The Conversation.

that in Yemen, it is possible for a globally just Green New Deal to imagine the transition of arms industry jobs, skills and resources to renewables and other non-military outputs. Countries and regional blocks of countries who are using their power to negotiate preferential trading terms for the corporations registered within their territories, would be forced to consider more equitable terms and humane outputs.

Dismantling green colonialism
HAMZA HAMOUCHENE

Hamza Hamouchene is the North Africa Programme Coordinator for Transnational Institute, based in London, UK.

> *2020 started with an unprecedented oil price crash, as Russia and Saudi Arabia vied to compete with US shale oil producers. The plunge in oil prices was unparalleled and drove straight into pandemic lockdowns. Oil prices reached negative values as some oil producers in the US paid buyers to take oil from them for lack of storage capacity. The impact was brutal among oil companies, especially in the high-cost US shale oil sector. As for oil-producing countries such as Algeria, Libya, Nigeria as well as Venezuela, Ecuador and Iraq, economic strain was added to already precarious economies with mounting budget deficits and a haemorrhaging of financial reserves.*
>
> *Against this backdrop, some wondered whether this signalled the end of the fossil fuel industry and oil dependency. Caution however must be exercised. Adam Hanieh perspicaciously warns that this juncture could be an opportunity for the oil majors to concentrate capital and centralise control of the industry by getting rid of smaller producers.[4] A transition away from fossil fuels really depends on our capacities to build effective political and economic alternatives.*
>
> *In the popular imagination, when we talk about energy, we talk about coal, oil and gas. Most of these resources (especially the latter*

---

4   Hanieh, Adam (2020). 'When oil markets go viral.' Verso Blog.

two) are extracted from the South. In fact, much of anything that is con-sumed in the North has been taken from the South, whether through agribusiness, intensive forestry, industrial fish farming, mass tourism and I would argue, even the renewable energy sector.[5] Set in motion from 1492 with the conquest of the Americas, this system is charac-terized by a belief that the resources of others are for the taking. Iraq and Libya warrant more attention here as they are the recent victims of the violence caused by fossil fuels and the western fighter jets and bombs that go searching for their abundance.[6] It lives on through debt, trade and investment structures that have seen limited benefits for the majority of people living in countries rich in mineral and metal wealth.

While certain Western governments portray themselves as pro-environment by banning fracking within their borders and setting carbon emission-reduction targets, they offer diplomatic support to multinationals registered in their territories, just as France supported Total to exploit shale resources in their former colony, Algeria.[7] This hand in glove relationship between multinational corporations and governments of the countries in which they're registered (usually in former colonies) continues. While Chinese companies increasingly appear in the world's largest companies (by revenue), they repeat colonial attitudes towards resources and labour while the remaining multinationals that make up that list appear disproportionately from the US (e.g. Walmart, ExxonMobil UnitedHealth and Chevron), and Europe (e.g. Royal Dutch Shell, Total, BP, Glencore). They profit from the labour and resources that make up their complex supply chains.

Sophie Chapelle and Olivier Petitjean. Shale gas: how Algerians rallied against the Regime and Foreign Oil Companies. Multinationales. org. June 2016. Can be accessed here. ●

5 Hamouchene, Hamza (2019). 'Extractivisim and resistance in North Africa'. Transnational Institute.

6 Klein, Naomi (2016). 'Let Them Drown: The Violence of Othering in a Warming World'. London Review of Books.

7 Chapelle, Sophie and Olivier Petitjean (2016). 'Shale gas: how Algerians rallied against the Regime and Foreign Oil Companies', trans. Susanna Gendall. Multinationals Observatory.

Decarbonisation and Foreign Policy in the Middle East
DAVID WEARING

Dr. David Wearing is a Lecturer in Department Of International Relations at University Of Southampton, based in London, UK.

Like the major oil and gas corporations, airlines and car manufacturers, and perhaps those firms dealing in oil based products such as petrochemicals, plastics and fertiliser, the world's most powerful states have their own reasons for maintaining the carbon based economy. They represent an obstacle to decarbonisation every bit as formidable as ExxonMobil or Royal Dutch Shell.

That hydrocarbons are the lifeblood of the world economy means that the huge oil and gas reserves of the Middle East constitute a vital strategic prize. This is why the region has been the site of such sustained and violent inter-state conflict since the end of the Second World War. Moreover, with a rising China dependent on oil and gas imports from the Persian Gulf, where US power continues to dominate, Washington derives enormous structural power from current patterns of energy production and consumption.

The profits generated from the sale of oil and gas are also of great interest to states as well as corporations. The sovereign wealth of the major oil producers is one of the most significant sources of liquid capital in the world. The combined sovereign wealth of Saudi Arabia and the other Gulf Arab monarchies amounts to $2.9tn, while corporate and private wealth in those states adds up to a further $3tn. These "petrodollars" can be "recycled" to the benefit of Western states.

Petrodollar investment in the US, UK and France is made by the Gulf states as much in the interests of regime security as in the expectation of a favourable economic return. The links between Western finance and the Gulf Arab monarchies developed in the context of imperialism, where monarchical rule has been able to entrench itself and fend off more progressive social forces thanks to the decisive backing of Western states.

This is even more obviously true in respect of the major arms purchases made by the Gulf monarchs, which in turn equip the Western powers to continue their role as the monarchies' protectors. If Western states are to adopt the Green New Deal policies needed to ensure our survival, they themselves will need to be radically transformed. ●

In the next piece, Justin Podur, provocatively asks whether it will be possible to shake off the imperial and racist roots of the original New Deal and poses whether we might, instead, seek to operationalise five year plans that aim to undo a violent past.

Leaving behind the racist and imperialist baggage of the original New Deal
JUSTIN PODUR

Justin Podur is Associate Professor in Faculty Of Environmental And Urban Change at York University, based in Toronto, Canada.

The original New Deal, and its champion, Franklin D. Roosevelt, are credited with saving the US economy from the Great Depression and, perhaps, saving the country from socialism. The story is told in Stan Cox's new book The Green New Deal and Beyond where he powerfully narrates the story[8]:

In 1932, US unemployment was at 24%. The New Deal started by designating $3.3 billion for public works, an amount larger than the entire federal budget 3 years before. Roosevelt created new agencies to try to steer private industry into a gentle, voluntary form of economic

---

8   Cox, Stan (2020). The Green New Deal and Beyond: Ending the Climate Emergency While We Still Can. City Lights Publishers, p.9.

planning. In 1935, the Supreme Court struck down one of these initiatives (the National Recovery Act), but the same year, the New Dealers started a Works Progress Administration (WPA) that hired eight million unemployed Americans to build public infrastructure.

The New Deal also took place in a time of unremitting White terror towards Black people in the US South. New Deal programs helped cement racial inequalities. Federal relief agencies paid locally prevailing wages, allowing lower wages in the US South. Black sharecroppers' government benefits were kept by their white landlords. White plantation owners would receive federal compensation for cotton extracted from land, and then turn around and evict the Black tenants that worked the land anyway. Social Security did not cover farm workers or domestic workers - the occupations that employed two thirds of Black workers. The Federal Housing Administration (FHA) required banks to perpetuate segregation: "If a neighbourhood is to retain stability, it is necessary that properties shall continue to be occupied by the same social and racial classes," the FHA underwriting manual instructed.

Despite this, the New Deal faced elite opposition, and so Roosevelt reduced stimulus funds by 25% between 1936-8. Unemployment went back up to 19%. In the end, the New Deal was not the answer to the Depression. That answer came in the form of a war. First supplying Europe, then sending the US military to World War Two. According to Patrick Renshaw (quoted by Cox), the US spent $321 billion on World War Two, more than its total spending from 1790-1940. During World War Two, unemployment went down to 1.2%.

The New Deal took place in the age of imperialism. India, Africa, much of southeast Asia, were colonies. The Philippines and Cuba were US possessions. Other lands that the US had taken - Puerto Rico and Hawaii - still are. In the Arab world, the British sponsored the House of Saud, dismantled and subordinated the economies of the Levant and Egypt. By the time of the New Deal, the US empire was pushing the British empire out of the fossil fuel-rich Middle East. In 1945 Roosevelt met the Saudi king at Great Bitter Lake in the Suez canal, moving Saudi Arabia into the US' system. What economists Jonathan Nitzan and Shimshon Bichler call the "weapondollar-petrodollar" global economy was established.

Illustration by Tomekah George

The Saudi dictatorship would ensure that the price of oil would favour the US, which would get back what it paid for the oil in weapons sales. The hundreds of billions of dollars of sales of military hardware would be conducted in US dollars, the reserve currency of all the world, which enabled the US to print money and accumulate wealth at the expense of every other country.

While ending facism through World War Two was necessary, it paved the way for a US economy built on conflict. Underpinning this system is a regime of permanent US warfare that has killed millions in the decades since the New Deal, including the dropping of nuclear bombs on Japan, the high-tech destruction and aerial bombardment of Korea, Vietnam, Grenada, Panama, Iraq, Yugoslavia, Afghanistan, Palestine, Lebanon, Libya, Syria, Yemen and other countries, covert operations in every country in the world, and the imminent threat of nuclear catastrophe. It is an empire based on endless war and fossil fuels.

Climate change is one of its life-destroying consequences. In making the US the wealthiest society in human history, the stimulus of the New Deal played a much smaller role than the stimulus of World War Two. The long-term wealth of the US was guaranteed not by either stimulus, but by the consolidation of a global empire with the US at its centre.

Given this context, can the New Deal be divested of its racist and imperialist baggage and reinvented to save the world from climate catastrophe? At the end of The Green New Deal and Beyond, Cox suggests a series of ways that a Green New Deal could include justice for the financially and energy-impoverished peoples of the world. This starts not with greening the US military, as Elizabeth Warren suggested on the US campaign trail, but with disarming and dismantling it, as well as the militarized police in the US, both of which are disastrous fossil fuel consumers while also being implicated in persistent human rights abuses. Protecting and expanding Indigenous land bases will not only redress some of the horrors of colonialism, but also reduce carbon emissions from land use. In some places - like Haiti or the Democratic Republic of Congo - the use of energy will actually have to increase for there to be any economic justice.

If we are going to have to discard baggage one way or another, internationalists might find more interesting experiences and tools from a study of the Five Year Plans of communist China and the Soviet Union and of India when it was socialist. These countries' economies and polities have had many flaws, and their planning processes have had many errors, all of which have been amplified by Western propaganda as efficiently as the West's colonial genocides and massacres have been minimized. It may be productive to study how vast, poor countries devastated by imperialism tried to plan for development within severe constraints - including a hostile empire. ●

Illustration by Molly Crabapple

9. WHO PAYS? DEBT, REPARATIONS, AND ACCOUNTABILITY

Climate change harms are here. This chapter explores who must pay for the impacts already occurring, as well as efforts to limit warming to as close as 1.5°C through a rapid, democratic and justice-centred green transition. This means paying for adaptation projects designed to effectively increase resilience to inevitable climate change. It also means repairing the consequences of extreme weather and slow-onset events like sea level rise or desertification, and enabling global decarbonisation.

What climate change harms need repairing?

The five hottest years on record have all taken place since 2015. This has taken a significant toll on older people, carers, and day-labourers who work outside. Deadly heatwaves and vector-borne diseases proliferate, and rural populations must travel ever further for clean water. More severe droughts (leading to desertification, land degradation and food and nutritional insecurity) are being caused by a confluence of rising temperatures, erratic rainfall, and rising sea level.[1] Reduced crop yields resulting from these droughts lead to hunger and poverty, and extreme temperatures affect habitats, pushing species to extinction, and farmers to untold hardship. These factors interact with pre-existing political instability, conflict, displacement, migration, economic exclusion.

The cyclones, hurricanes and typhoons that we see today are bringing noticeably heavier rainfall, causing more flooding, stronger winds, and bigger storm surges. Existing insurance schemes are insufficient for the scale and frequency of such events. In November 2013, Typhoon Haiyan[2] devastated the Tacloban region of the Philippines. It led to 6,000 deaths, damage or destruction to one million homes, and four million people being displaced. Of the approximately USD$10 billion of damages caused[3], only a small fraction was covered by insurance (between USD$300 – 700 million[4]). Insurance is not available for slow-onset events, nor where extreme weather events are becoming increasingly regular. Insurance also requires countries at the forefront of experiencing climate change impacts to pay for expensive premiums. In December 2019, the Philippines Human Rights Commission held that civil and criminal law may be leveraged against the largest carbon companies for materially increasing the risk of harm to its residents.[5]

In March 2019, Cyclone Idai struck Mozambique as well as Malawi and Zimbabwe. It was one of the strongest storms on record. Within weeks, Cyclone Kenneth, identified as the strongest cyclone in Mozambique's history, surprisingly hit the north of the country. Never, since records began[6] has Mozambique been hit by two such strong storms in one year. The cyclones left over two million people in need of humanitarian services, over 1 million children in need of humanitarian services, 648 people dead, and infrastructure

1   Ware, Joe and Katherine Kramer (2019). 'Hunger Strike: The climate and food vulnerability index.' ChristianAid.

2   Reid, Kathryn (2018). '2013 Typhoon Haiyan: Facts, FAQs and how to help.' World Vision.

3   OHCHR (2014). 'Typhoon Haiyan: UN human rights expert calls for urgent debt relief for reconstruction in the Philippines.' OHCHR UN.

4   Rupp, Lindsey (2013). 'Philippine Typhoon Haiyan's Cost to Insurers Estimated at $300-$700million: AIR.' Insurance Journal.

5   Amnesty International (2019). 'Philippines: Landmark decision by Human Rights Commission paves way for climate litigation.' Amnesty International.

6   Shaw, Diana (2019). 'Mozambique: urgent aid needed after Cyclone Kenneth.' Red Cross Blog.

destruction, displacement, the spread of cholera, and crop damage.[7] Cyclone Idai alone destroyed more than 1,720,000 acres of crops including corn, cassava, beans, rice and groundnuts such as peanuts. The hunger and poverty impacts were exacerbated by the fact that the cyclone arrived following a drought related to the El Niño period, during which normal tropical precipitation is disrupted, triggering extreme weather events. The latest Southern Africa Development Community's Food and Nutrition Security Report, shows that 41 million people are now hungry in Southern Africa, compared to 29.4 million people in 2018. Years of unpredictable weather, inconsistent harvests, storms are eroding gains made toward poverty eradication and improved health. Chronic malnutrition impedes the functional and cognitive development of children.[8]

The fallout from extreme climate events such as Cyclone Idai are unequivocally gendered. Women and girls are already often at a greater distance from water collection points, sanitation facilities and health centres, which may be in unsafe locations, exposing them to additional protection threats such as sexual and gender-based violence in times of crisis. With the destruction of health facilities, pregnant women have limited access to support for delivering their babies safely. Girls are more likely to miss out on school following the damage wrought to schools and learning materials following the cyclones.[9] Mozambique said it needed USD\$3.2 billion to recover[10] - yet, the IMF agreed an emergency loan of just USD\$118.2 million to Mozambique following Cyclone Idai.[11] The average person in the US emits 51 times more carbon than the average person in Mozambique.

In China, the June–July 2016 flooding that killed more than 833 people, destroyed upwards of 400,000 houses and displaced more than 6 million people was made significantly worse by human-caused climate change.[12] In the Caribbean, Hurricane Dorian - the most intense tropical cyclone to strike the

7   Shaw, Diana (2019). 'Record-breaking two cyclones hit Mozambique: urgent aid needed after Cyclone Kenneth.' Red Cross Blog.

8   CARE Press (2019). 'Cyclone Idai 6 months on: CARE issues dire warnings as studies show 41 million face hunger in Southern Africa.' CARE.

9   ReliefWeb (2019). 'From cyclone to food crisis: ensuring the needs of women and girls are prioritized in the Cyclone Idai and Kenneth responses.' ReliefWeb.

10 AP (2019). 'Mozambique seeks USD 3.2 billion to recover from cyclones.' Business-Standard.

11 Suffee, Zak (2019). 'IMF loan to Mozambique following Cyclone Idai "shocking indictment" of international community.' Jubilee Debt Campaign.

12 Climate Signals (2018). 'China Floods June-July 2016.' Climate Signals.

Bahamas in 2019 - showed both the US' intransigence to support through allowing temporary visas to survivors, and the ways in which similar intolerance is wielded from inside frontline countries as Haitian migrants disproportionately impacted by property damage were promptly deported.[13]

Globally, the impact of extreme natural disasters (whether or not linked to climate change) is equivalent to about USD£520 billion annually, and forces approximately 26 million people into poverty each year.[14] In 2019, 24.9 million people were newly displaced by about 1900 disasters across 140 countries and territories.[15] Climate change specific disasters are now occurring at a rate of one per week[16] and are set to cost at least $300 billion per year going forward.[17]

The IPCC's September 2019 Special Report on the Ocean and Cryosphere in a Changing Climate[18] concluded that warming oceans, melting ice, and rising sea levels are already affecting everything from coral reefs to the nearly 10% of the global population living in low-lying coastal areas—and negative impacts will greatly worsen in the future.[19]

Reparation in this context requires more than houses being built on new territory, money or assets. It will require a public acknowledgement about the true role of climate change and its key perpetrators, the universally enshrined right to dignified migration, and ways of remembering ancestral connections to lost land through creative arts.

As of 2015, the Global North is responsible for 92 percent of excess global CO2 emissions - the US and EU alone are responsible for 49 percent of total territorial CO2 emissions between 1850 and 2015.[20] The average CO2 emissions (metric tons per capita) of citizens in countries most vulnerable to climate change impacts, pales in comparison to the average emissions of a person in the US, Canada, Australia, or UK. The global poor – many of whom survive

13 Mahdawi, Arwa (2019). 'The plight of Hurricane Dorian evacuees offers a frightening vision of 'climate apartheid.' The Guardian.

14 The World Bank (2016). 'Breaking the link between extreme weather and extreme poverty.' The World Bank.

15 IDMC (2020). 'Global Report on Internal Displacement 2020.' IDMC.

16 Harvey, Fiona (2019). 'One climate crisis disaster happening every week, UN warns.' The Guardian.

17 Leahy, Stephen (2017). 'Hidden costs of climate change running hundreds of billions a year.' National Geographic.

18 IPCC (2019). 'Special Report on the Ocean and Cryosphere in a Changing Climate.' IPCC.

19 Mulder, Natasha (2019). 'Surviving climate change and migration in Bangladesh.' ActionAid.

20 Hickel, Jason (2020). 'Quantifying national responsibility for climate breakdown: an equality-based attribution approach for carbon dioxide emissions in excess of the planetary boundary.' The Lancet 4(9).

on less than USD$2 per day – generate almost no greenhouse gas emissions but are disproportionately impacted by climate change impacts. This is grotesquely unfair and requires a global response that is both reparative and proportional. These impacts also sit upon colonial extraction and continued trade and investment practices that left previous colonies in politically, socially and economically precarious positions. Indeed, colonialism fundamentally reconfigured the world economy: India's share of the global economy shrank from 27 to 3%, while the UK benefited by approximately USD$45 trillion from its colonial rule of the Indian subcontinent alone.[21] While China's share shrank from 35 to 7%, Europe's share exploded from 20 to 60%.[22]

The legacies and impacts of slavery, colonialism , discrimination and neo-liberal policies contribute to a deepening of climate change impacts. Colonial practices (such as producing sugar, coffee, rice, and cotton cultivation on large slave plantations continue) continue to be indicators for per capita levels of poverty today, while neoliberal trade policies have continued to perpetuate inequities. This is important, because climate change magnifies existing patterns of social and material inequality, in addition to inequities in economic and political agency.[23]

Even if we start responsibility from the industrial revolution - and not from 1492 - ActionAid, Christian Aid, War on Want and Friends of the Earth calculate that in order for a country like the UK to do its fair share to limit global warming to 1.5°C, it would have to reach net zero by 2030 and support at least the same level of emissions reductions in low-income countries overseas, in addition to enabling increased resilience and repairing loss and damage. It could undertake this support by: enabling sustainable energy access for all; promoting agroecological farming; stopping the public financing of fossil fuels' eliminating tropical deforestation from its supply chains; supporting sustainable urbanization; scaling up public climate financing for decarbonisation initiatives; providing additional public climate financing for climate adaptation and resilience, and repairing the consequences of climate change impacts already occurring through social protection and access to public services.[24] Universal passports for those fleeing inhabitable lands could also be issued

21 Hickel, Jason (2018). 'How Britain stole $45 trillion from India.' Al Jazeera.

22 Hickel, Jason (2015). 'Enough of aid - let's talk reparations.' The Guardian.

23 Bruhn, Miriam (2010). 'Did yesterday's patterns of colonial exploitation determine today's patterns of poverty?.' World Bank Blogs.

24 Christian Aid et al., (2020). 'The UK's Climate Fair Share To Limit Global Warming to 1.5 degrees.' Christian Aid.

with supportive and welcoming re-settlement processes.

In order to do this, progressive redistribution is essential - with the recognition that across and within countries, the highest per capita of carbon emissions are attributable to the wealthiest people. Those subjected to housing shortages, food deserts, health inequalities, disproportionate exposure to environmental hazards and energy poverty in the UK cannot be expected to pay as much as the CEOs of UK-based fossil fuel giants towards funding local and global initiatives. Those taking multiple holidays, consuming luxury goods and services, and driving in luxury cars have a far greater responsibility and capability.

Individual emissions generally parallel disparities of income and wealth. While the world's richest 10% cause 50% of emissions, they also claim 52% of the world's wealth. The world's poorest 50% contribute approximately 10% of

Illustration by Tomekah George

global emissions and receive about 8% of global income. Wealth increases adaptive capacity, meaning those most responsible for climate change are relatively insulated from its impacts.

Moving away from state accountability, it is also essential to note that a relatively small number of global corporations are directly responsible for the bulk of emissions. The 2017 Carbon Majors Study[25] found that just one hundred fossil fuel companies generate 71% of anthropogenic greenhouse gas emissions. Electricity producers, metals and engineering consortia, car makers, construction companies, petrochemicals and agriculture giants are among the greatest consumers of the energy generated.

In the 1980s, oil companies like Exxon and Shell carried out internal assessments of the carbon dioxide released by fossil fuels, and forecast the planetary consequences of these emissions, including the inundation of entire low-lying countries and regions, disappearance of specific ecosystems, destructive floods and water stress causing unprecedented global change. [26]The same companies funded misinformation campaigns to enable business as usual.

Chevron, Exxon, BP and Shell together are behind more than 10% of the world's carbon emissions since 1966. They originated in the Global North, and its governments continue to provide them with financial subsidies and tax breaks. According to the CSO Equity Review Coalition, state subsidies for fossil fuels are almost double the USD$140 billion spent on subsidies to renewable energy - and increase to USD$4.7 trillion when indirect subsidies are included.[27] States and corporations must do more to give us any chance to meet the '1.5°C to stay alive' ambition.[28]

Litigation which challenges state handouts to fossil fuel companies,

25 CDP (2017). 'The Carbon Majors Database: CDP Carbon Majors Report 2017'. CDP.

26 Hall, Shannon (2015). 'Exxon knew about climate change almost 40 years ago'. Scientific American.

27 CSO Equity Review (2019). 'Can climate change fuelled loss and damage ever be fair?'. CSO Equity Review Coalition.

28 Sealey-Huggins, Leon (2017). '"1.5 to stay alive": climate change, imperialism and justice for the Caribbean'. Third world Quarterly 38(11), p.2444-2463.

Illustration by Tomekah George

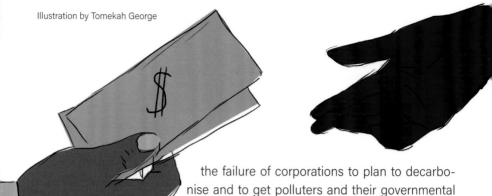

the failure of corporations to plan to decarbonise and to get polluters and their governmental
enablers to pay for current climate change impacts
is burgeoning throughout the world. The Netherlands
v. Urgenda Foundation case[29] was a watershed moment for the climate justice movement, forcing the state to
do more to meet its fair share of action, and give us a chance of
meeting Paris Agreement ambitions. Using similar mechanisms, children
are seeking intergenerational justice[30] and Peruvian farmers demanding fiscal
contributions for the cost of flood defenses in our already warmed world.[31]

A globally just Green New Deal would require reparations. This includes
reparations owed not only due to disproportionate greenhouse gas emissions,
but also the unfair trade and investment regimes and economic policies that
have curtailed the potential to protect people and planet over profit. Reparation would require debts to be cancelled (removing onerous loan conditions)
and the structures of unequal trade and investment be dismantled and rebuilt
more equitably. Reparation would require a transition from competition to cooperation, and centre the undoing of the systems of oppression that put some
communities disproportionately on the frontline of climate change impacts. It
would mean moving to re-using, sharing and consuming less but living well,
with abundant access to education, healthcare, housing, arts, clean water
and food, and a sustainable environment for current and future generations. It
means repairing climate harms.

29 Climate Case Chart (2015). 'Urgenda Foundation v. State of the Netherlands.' Climate Case Chart.

30 Sanson, Ann V. and Susie E. L. Burke (2019). 'Climate change and children: An issue of intergenerational
justice.' Children and Peace, p. 343-362.

31 Nugent, Ciara (2018). 'Climate change could destroy this Peruvian farmer's home. Now he's suing a
European energy company for damages.' Time.

Luciano Lliuya v. RWE AG: litigating for climate justice
ROXANA BALDRICH

Roxana Baldrich was, until recently, Policy Advisor For Climate Risk Management at Germanwatch, based in Bonn, Germany

A Peruvian small-scale farmer and mountain guide is taking bold steps for climate justice

Saúl Luciano Lliuya v. RWE AG is the first climate change lawsuit in which a court found (in November 2017) that a private company could potentially be held liable for climate damages from its emissions,[32] allowing the case to progress to the evidentiary stage. With support of the environmental NGO Germanwatch and the foundation Stiftung Zukunftsfähigkeit, Peruvian small-scale farmer and mountain guide Saúl Luciano Lliuya decided to take his fate into his own hands and do something about the climate risks that he and his community are facing. In 2015, he sued the German energy giant RWE, the biggest single emitter of CO_2 in Europe. He wants the company to assume its share of responsibility for the adverse impacts of climate change. In this concrete case, "adverse impacts" means that, due to climate-induced glacial retreat, a glacial lake above the Andean city of Huaraz has grown in size and threatens to overflow or even break its dam. The plaintiff's property along with large parts of the city are at risk of a devastating flood that would affect around 50,000 people. Saúl Luciano requests the court to determine that RWE is liable, proportionate to its historical GHG emissions, to cover the expenses for appropriate safety precautions. This could mean, for example, paying part of the cost of a much bigger dam and/or a pumping system at the glacial lake.

The plaintiff himself explains his motivation for the lawsuit as follows:

---

32 Toussaint, Patrick (2020). 'Loss and damage and climate litigation: The case for greater interlinkage.' Reciel: Review of European, Comparative & International Environmental Law.'

Every day, I see the glaciers melting and the lakes in the mountains growing. For us in the valley, the threat is immense. We cannot simply wait and see what happens. For me, RWE is partly responsible for the risks that threaten us in Huaraz. According to scientific studies, the lake above my hometown is growing because of accelerated glacier melting. RWE is one of the world's biggest emitters. But so far, these companies have not assumed any responsibility for the consequences of their emissions. You don't have to be a legal scholar to see that this is wrong. That is why we demand that they now at least install flood protection at our glacier lake. And even better, that they should stop contaminating the climate in the future so that all people can survive. We used to be powerless, but we aren't anymore. This is about our protection and about justice.

Saúl Luciano is aware that his plight is not an isolated one. He hopes that his lawsuit will set a precedent and benefit others who are threatened or impacted by climate change. The final goal of climate change lawsuits is the establishment of global corporate legal accountability as well as global political responsibility for climate change. In order to contribute to that goal, Saúl Luciano and his lawyer wanted to create a 'test case' that would be replicable in many other countries. Therefore, their claim is based on the general nuisance provision under German civil law (§1004 BGB). Nuisance is one of the oldest and most widely used causes of action, and provisions similar to §1004 exist in many other jurisdictions. What is more, it can be used both, when there is a risk of nuisance or actual nuisance. Applied to climate change lawsuits, this means that it can be used to ask for the financing of adaptation measures, or for compensation for climate harms.

While the facts of the "Huaraz Case" are still being evaluated in the ongoing evidentiary phase,[33] the court's recognition that a private company could potentially be held liable for the climate change related damages of its emissions marks a significant development in law. This might inspire other plaintiffs to make similar claims, or other judges to take similar decisions. ●

---

33 Climate Case Chart (2015). 'Luciano Lliuya v. RWE AG'. Sabin Center for Climate Change Law.

While corporations must be held to account for the consequences of their emissions in remote villages, far from where they operate, they must also pay reparations for their subjection of violence in communities where they directly extract:

Corporate profiteering in the Niger delta
KEN HENSHAW

Ken Henshaw works for We The People, based in Port Harcourt, Nigeria.

From Corporate Profiteering and State Repression to a Just New Deal in Nigeria's Oil Niger Delta

From the start, the business of oil extraction in Nigeria's Niger Delta operated as a deadly mix of corporate profiteering and state backed repression. From the early 1950s when oil exploitation gained momentum, the relations of production have followed the patterns of commerce established by western traders and colonial powers, essentially characterized by a wedlock of rapacious profits facilitated by military/armed repression. For instance, in 1895 - over 60 years before the commencement of crude oil export from Nigeria - the British Navy burnt down Brass, a thriving Niger Delta trading site, to secure a palm oil monopoly for the British owned Royal Niger Company. About 2000 died in the process. Upon independence in 1960, the substitution of the Union Jack for independent Nigeria's green and white flag did not alter the character of the oil business. Nigeria's sovereign security forces continued in the same vain.

At no time in the decision-making chain on oil extraction were the indigenous people of the Nigeria Delta, in whose farmlands, rivers and creeks crude oil is found, consulted, considered or valued. From the start, the partnership was between state and companies, and the drivers were always profit and plunder by any means necessary. The history of oil exploitation is littered with corporate and state abuses against communities whose only crime is demanding a new and fairer deal.

In 1990, the people of Umuechem community where Shell has extracted crude oil since 1958, went on a peaceful march demanding a new deal from the company and the Nigerian government. Shell had promised roads, hospitals, schools, electricity and job opportunities when they arrived in the community thirty years earlier. Fast forward three decades, none of the promises had been kept. In its place, the farming and fishing community was exposed to pollution, land grabs and loss of livelihoods. In response to the peaceful protest of the Umuechem people, Shell called in tactical units of the Nigerian police who burnt everything, killing 100 people in the Umuechem massacre. Nobody has been held to account. Shell continues to extract crude oil on its terms in Umuechem.

In the same period, the same level of state supported repression was unleashed on the Ogoni people. This time it was the Nigerian army acting in the interests of Shell. Again, the people had peacefully demanded a new deal from Shell and the Nigerian state. Thousands of community members were killed, raped and exiled. The leadership of the Movement for the Survival of Ogoni People, which included Ken Saro Wiwa, were executed on the recommendations of a stage-managed military tribunal.

In defense of oil companies and their reckless extraction, the Nigerian government continues to attack communities in the Niger Delta using special units of the armed forces. In November 1999, the military killed 2,500 people in the village of Odi. In 2005, 17 persons were killed in Odioma for demanding community benefits. In 2008, Twon Brass, Epebu, Agge and Uzere communities were attacked. In 2019 alone, at least 3 communities in the Niger Delta were attacked and burnt by the military.

Today, after 6 decades of oil extraction, the Niger Delta is one of the most polluted, poverty stricken and militarized places on earth. For the indigenous people of the region, every attempt to define a new deal has consistently resulted in cruelty and death. For them, any kind of transition must depart from the rather narrow fixation on jobs; it must address the consequences of decades of reckless and mindless oil extraction. A just transition and a new deal has to repair the ecological disaster occasioned by oil pollution in the Niger Delta which has eliminated the livelihoods of the people. A just transition must seek to provide justice for the countless victims of oil company inspired and state sanctioned abuses. A just transition must include reparations to the people of the Niger Delta for the years of mindless expropriation.

Beyond being green and environment friendly, the new deal has to be people inspired and centered. It must be a deal fashioned by the people, within the context of their reality and addressing the peculiarity of their needs. Every previous deal has been the product of the wedlock between oil-multinationals and governments, fixated on profits and enforced with terror. ●

In this next piece we turn to action. In response to finding out that BP was sponsoring an exhibition on Assyrian leader Ashurbanipal's empire, ruled from ancient Iraq, Yasmin Younis joined an activist theatre group to 'take over' the museum and highlight BP's campaign to 'artwash' its history. A history which has seen BP executives aiming to ensure they "get a fair slice of the action for UK companies in a post-Saddam Iraq" despite experts foreseeing thousands of civilian deaths.

Building a climate movement that can reshape foreign policy
YASMIN YOUNIS

Yasmin Younis is a First-Year Law Student at St Louis University School Of Law in St Louis, Missouri.

Global movements see young people utilizing their power by voicing their grievances, organizing in different youth-run climate change organizations,[34] and using all available platforms to make their demands heard and spread. Polluters Out's (PO) twitter campaign

34 Wikler, Maia (2019). '5 Youth-Led Climate Justice Groups Helping to Save the Environment.' Teen Vogue.

showed the power of social media in garnering the attention of BP's directors and CEO.[35] PO argues that the campaign's pressure helped start a conversation with the very leaders of the corporation, which opened seemingly unimaginable doors.

From petitions to campaigns to evidence of the environmental harms produced by such corporations' failures to administer environmentally conscious practices, action is required. Movements can target corporations by disrupting their ability to recruit and retain talent as perfectly exemplified by the Black Lives Matter (BLM) movement's #PullUpOrShutUp campaign[36] which globally calls out corporations on racial inequity and discrimination. Politicians and governments brush over climate activists because they don't find their demands realistic and credible and the fossil fuel industry has too much influence; however, if movements can control the conversation through the industries themselves, then will we see the beginnings of policy change. ●

Countries in the Global North as the early industrializers - as well as fossil fuel companies and the agro-industry - have a unique responsibility pay towards meeting our rapid decarbonisation ambitions, and to ensure communities least responsible for climate change are not left to fend off the impacts of it without adequate adaptation measures, social protection and reparation. In addition, though, trade and investment regimes that entrench inequalities and create dependence, must also be left behind. So, too, must debt and a system of granting loans that appears humanitarian but is, in fact, toxic. As Black Lives Matter protests abound, we are also inspired to re-think the concept of when time starts running for culpability to pay towards climate impacts. For so long the debate has been between 1850 and much later dates, all the way to 1990. Climate change multiples inequalities set in motion through colonialism, slavery, patriarchy. Why, then, would reparations to repair climate change impacts, decarbonise and adapt, not seek to transform the social vulnerabilities that deepen our crisis? Climate change harms magnify existing patterns of social, material, economic and political inequality and exclusion. Groups and peoples

35 Fallahi, Isabella (2020). 'Polluters Out is a New Youth Coalition Pushing for Divestment from Fossil Fuels'. Teen Vogue.

36 Abraham, Tameka (2020). 'Sharon Chuter on the #PullUpOrShutUp Campaign and Real Change in the Beauty Industry'. Byrdie.

already experiencing social, material, political and economic exclusion (for example, on the basis of poverty, gender, age, indigenous or minority status and disability, national or social origin, birth or other status) are disproportionately negatively impacted by climate change harms. A Global Green New Deal can have a transformative impact if the root causes of exclusion are redressed and repaired, and resources are redistributed to allow for universal flourishing in a low carbon future.

Colonial Debt and Reparations
BROULAYE BAGAYOKO
Translated by Romane Prigent.

Broulaye Bagayoko is a Permanent Secretary for Coalition
Of Alternative Debt And Development (Cadtm Africa in
Bamako, Mali.

> *Slavery, beginning as early as the 16th century, seized thousands of capable African families. Gold, which represented the most significant African natural resource, lined the pockets of French banks. Jules Ferry, former president of the French Council, declared in 1885: "the colonies represent, for the wealthy countries, the most profitable capital placement". Many African countries, upon earning their independence, were left with imposed colonial debts transferred to newly-established independent governments*
>
> *Fast forward and during the Cold War, loans enticed African countries to steer away from socialist policies and rewarded corrupt African governments for creating welcoming environments for foreign investment in place of focusing on the well-being of citizens.*
>
> *Tied-aid has become emblematic in the African continent. For instance, a country may loan 1 million CFA francs to Mali while imposing a (albeit reduced) interest rate. The loan is given on the condition that Mali purchase 1 million CFA francs worth of goods from this same - supposedly "donor" country. This ultimately results in indirectly subsidising large companies in the Global North, and charging the African people the interest rates for the burden of doing so.*

Any historic "investment" in roads, railroads, harbours was intended to facilitate the export of African natural resources to Europe's metropolitan centres. Tunisia even went into debt to buy its own land back from its colonisers. While slaves have never received reparations for being sold, the British government was - in 2015 - still paying slave owners reparations for their lost property upon the abolition of slavery. Southern countries, rich in minerals, are forced to export more and more mineral resources to sustain the industries of developed countries. The looting and exploitation of colonised economies played a role in the underdevelopment of these countries, which we call "economic migrants". Most colonised countries never recovered from this pillaging.

France threatened Haiti with another military invasion and the reestablishment of slavery if it did not pay a compensation of 150 million gold francs. The World Bank of the 1950's supported the colonial powers through loan grants. Certain conditions attached to the loans were imposed on the borrowing nations, including population control measures which disproportionate targeted poor women. Belgium transferred its debt to the World Bank, incurred by the Belgian colonial government, to Congo. Congo received 120 million dollars of loans, of which 105.4 million dollars were spent in Belgium.

"Colonisation is a crime against humanity" stated Emmanuel Macron in February 2017 in Alger. Indeed, but it is not enough to acknowledge it: these crimes must be tried and repaired for. The first step would be to recognise that the countries considered as "indebted" are in fact the creditors and to correct this particular view of the world. The second step consists in paying reparations for these human, economic, and ecological crimes committed in history, consistent with the call made by Thomas Sankara,[37] President of Burkina Faso, on 29 July 1987, at the 25th African Unity Organisation Summit in Ethiopia. ●

---

37 Sankara, Thomas (2018). 'A United Front Against Debt (1987)'. Viewpoint Magazine.

Debt cancellation and reparations - Southern movement perspectives
LIDY NACPIL

Lidy Nacpil is a Coordinator for Asian Peoples' Movement On Debt And Development, based in Manila, Philippines.

Debt servicing has put incredible constraints on public spending for essential services or "social protection" in the Global South, but it also has done a lot more harm than that. Illegitimate debts, debt servicing and conditionalities all straightjacket us. This injustice sits upon the historical, social, and ecological debts owed to the peoples of the South, since colonialism, and they form the major bases for our call for reparations.

First let's talk about debt. The so-called "debts of the South" have grown steadily, and during some periods quite dramatically, over the years. The major debt relief programs of international financial institutions and bilateral lender of the past two decades - the Highly Indebted Poor Countries (HIPC) debt relief program launched in 1996 and ënhanced in 1990, and the Multilateral Debt Relief Initiative (MDRI) announced in 2005 - were heavily criticized for offering too little relief for too few countries.

In fact, a lot of the debts covered by HIPC were not being serviced, thus debt relief mainly functioned as a way of clearing up creditors' books from uncollectible loans. In addition, these initiatives exacerbated other problems by requiring compliance with conditionalities including cuts and caps on social spending and freeze on salaries of public employees including teachers. Furthermore, these initiatives may have provided some ease in debt payments and reduction in outstanding debts but beneficiary countries considered to be no longer severely indebted had much less access to highly concessional loans and instead were compelled to borrow from financial markets with much higher interest rates and increase their domestic borrowings.

The Covid-19 pandemic brings into sharp focus once again the problem of debt and the urgent need for real solutions and not just *temporary, very short term relief. Unfortunately the offers as of the time of this writing from international financial institutions led by the IMF and from bilateral lenders led by the G20 again involve very little relief for too few countries. The IMF announced its debt relief initiative in April 2020 with $500 million to be provided through its Catastrophe Containment and Relief Trust to cover the debt payments for 6 months in 2020 of twenty-nine countries considered to be the poorest and most vulnerable. The G20 announced within the same month, the Debt Service Suspension Initiative which involves simply a delay of debt service due from 1 May 2020 to 31 December 2020. Countries eligible to apply only include those in the list of the World Bank's International Development Agency (IDA) and the United Nations' list of Least Developed Countries - a total of 76 countries. The amount of debt service to be suspended if all eligible countries apply and all G20 countries participate is only about USD$11 billion. The G20 offer only covers 3.65% of all the debt service payments to be made in 2020 by developing countries.*

It must be noted that the debt service being canceled and/or suspended are only those to be paid to official creditors. Nearly half of public external debt is owed to private lenders. Many campaigns and movements - south and north - are calling for deeper, wider cancel- ation (and not just suspension) of public debt payments for a much bigger number of countries and for a longer period of at least 4 years as an immediate response to the pandemic and the economic crisis, and in addition for decisive steps to be taken for more comprehensive and lasting solutions to the debt problem, including total and uncon- ditional cancelation of outstanding debt stock and changes in the international financial architecture and borrowing and lending policies to prevent the re-accumulation of debt.

One of the key obstacles to debt solutions is how a debt crisis or debt distress is defined. For a long time creditors have held the view that there is a global debt crisis when many countries are not making their debt payments in full and on time. And countries are in debt distress if they are experiencing difficulties in servicing their debts. From the perspective and experience of peoples of the South - we have been in a permanent debt crisis, as debt payments continue to occupy a significant share of public spending and prioritized over vital needs such as basic services and economic policies that promote social justice, address poverty and inequality, build climate resilience and address loss and damage associated with climate change harms, and pave the way for equitable and post carbon development.

Debt injustice is more than the impact on public spending for the well-being and rights of people and communities, and more than the economic vulnerability to exogenous shocks. Loans, access to credit and debt relief have long been used as leverage to impose policy conditionalities, and this practice continues in various guises. The impact of many of these conditionalities, including tight austerity measures and privatization of essential services, are just as worse if not even worse than the debt problem.

Many debts peddled by lenders and incurred by governments in the name of their people were not actually used for the real benefit of people and many loan-financed projects have actually been harmful for communities and the environment. And yet these illegitimate debts are paid using peoples' money. Calls to address illegitimate debts as a priority must be renewed.

At the same time, the debt problem must be seen from a broader and historical view, in order to pave the way for strategic, just, fair and long lasting solutions The problem of the debt is a consequence of a long history of colonial and neo-colonial plunder of the resources and wealth of the South. It is not a coincidence that the first lenders to most southern countries were their colonizers, purportedly as part of the assistance and solutions to the impoverishment in the South. And this justification to massive lending and borrowing continues to this day through international financial institutions that continue the same work.

We are incapable of generating wealth - much of our countries' wealth - natural resources as well as wealth generated by our hard-working people - leave our countries in the form of illicit financial flows, capital flight, profit repatriation, interest payments on unsustainable and illegitimate debts, losses from underpriced exports and overpriced imports and unfair trade relations. The wealth that stays inside our countries is mostly controlled by elites and big corporations. This is borne by hard facts - on balance, there is a net outflow of resources from the south to the north. This requires structural reparations for Southern nations.

One of the biggest myths that continue to be perpetuated is that we lack wealth and capital, justifying the overzealous pursuit of loans on the part of many Southern governments, and the supply driven lending, unfair trade arrangements, and invasion of our economies and markets by northern and international elites, their financial institutions and their corporations. What we must fight for is not just debt cancellation but reparations, for the historical social, economic, ecological and climate debt owed to our people. And we must wage this fight as part of a broader struggle to transform the fundamentally flawed system that has been built on and perpetuated injustice and inequality in various dimensions, while devastating our people and our planet. ●

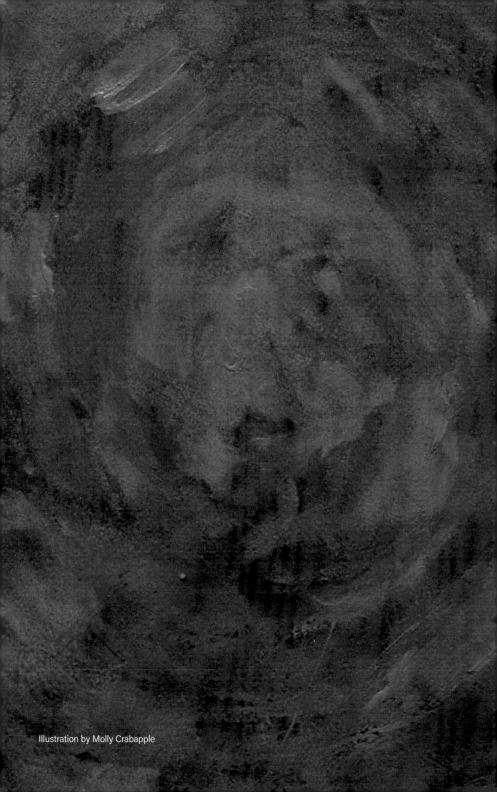

Illustration by Molly Crabapple

10. EPILOGUE

Avi Lewis

Avi Lewis is a Co-Founder of The Leap, and lives on the unceded territory of the shíshálh (Sechelt) and skwxwú7mesh (Squamish) nations in British Columbia, Canada.

This little book is a big deal.

Its pages amplify a global chorus of hard-won wisdom. Each section rings like a bell, with calls to action grounded in community, speaking clearly in the shared air, the enveloping atmosphere of resistance.

European and North American climate activism has been electrified by the emergence of the Green New Deal, which has rapidly shifted the terrain of political possibility – bringing forward solutions at speed and scale, to confront not just the planetary emergency, but the compounding crises of gaping inequality, white supremacy, and pandemic.

But just as each crisis is nested in the pre-existing conditions that gave rise to and exacerbate it, so must proposals like the GND ground their tender new roots in the rich soil of the movements that came before it. In this case, into the whole earth: the movements for global justice.

To be clear: it would be unconscionable to fight for a massive build-out of green public housing, clean mass transit, and renewable energy in the rich communities of the Global North if that process simply unleashed a whirlwind of extraction and exploitation in frontline communities in the Global South. That might be a Green Deal for some – but there would certainly be nothing new about who benefits and who pays the price.

On the other hand, the prospect of such a transformation that is led by, and accountable to, social movement and Indigenous leadership around the entire planet – that would be a new deal indeed, and the prospect is thrilling. It is an invitation to begin the life-saving work of repair.

In our short film, Message from the Future II: The Years of Repair, we allow ourselves to imagine what would get us to the starting line. The cascading uprisings, the rent strikes and essential worker movements that must arise and explode across borders, lifting the raised fist of solidarity to the rusty iron fist of oppression. This vision is not a prediction, but a rough sketch, a map drawn in the colours of a liberatory imagination. And so we also imagine the treasure on that map: the territory under repair.

On a material level, it's a picture of an economy that places high value on repairing stuff, to quiet the endless sucking sound of consumerism. This kind of repair must rest, of course, on a much more structural one: repairing basic human rights to infrastructure, safety nets, truly universal public services.

Most importantly, though, it means repairing relationships. And that involves both truth and reparations. First, making visible the ongoing flows of colonial extraction and accumulation; then, reversing them. Overturning the very logic of debt. Halting the indefensible transfer of wealth from South to North, then reversing the jet stream of extraction so that resources, technologies, medicine and more, start flowing the other way.

And there is an even deeper form of repair to which we are called: we need to re-pair. To re-connect ourselves as a global community. To draw back the guillotine's blade that severed us from each other, from traditional wisdom, from the web of life. This re-pairing is the work ahead – first hearing and seeing each other, connecting our struggles and our stories, ultimately knitting together a movement of movements that can dream justice into being.

In a historical moment of epic crisis and equal possibility, the whisper of a genuinely Global Green New Deal can, and must, build to a roar.